Born in Brooklyn. . . .
Raised in the CAV!

Freeholder Terry Duffy,
Was great meeting you.
Thanks for supporting
our Veterans.

[signature]

Born in Brooklyn. . . .
Raised in the CAV!

John E Flanagan
SABER Blue 37

John E. Flanagan

To order additional copies of this book, contact:
Xlibris Corporation
1-888-7-XLIBRIS
www.Xlibris.com
Orders@Xlibris.com

Contents

Chapter One: Fairy Tale or War Story 9

Chapter Two: God Bless you. 11

Chapter Three:
   B Troop 1st/ 9th is a long way from Brooklyn 18

Chapter Four: Reception Station 32

Chapter Five: Fort Wolters 46

Chapter Six: Best laid plans of mice and men. 50

Chapter Seven:
   Fort Rucker—The Home of Army Aviation 62

Chapter Eight: Good-bye USA 71

Chapter Nine: Welcome to the Blue Lift 83

Chapter Ten: An Khe—Dave Bressam 144

Chapter Eleven: LZ Two Bits 151

Chapter Twelve: Chu Lai 174

Chapter Thirteen:
   Good-bye Americal—Hello Camp Evans 206

Chapter Fourteen: We gotta get out of this place—
   if it's the last thing we ever do. 226

Acknowledgements 237

To the men—pilots, crew chiefs, Blues, gunners, scout
observers, mechanics, cooks, and clerks—
of Bravo Troop, 1st Squadron, 9th Cavalry
who every day set the standard for heroic performance in
battle.

And

To my big brother, Dave,—my #1 Fan—with love, hugs and
prayers.

3825-FLAN

Chapter One

Fairy Tale or War Story

The difference between a fairy tale and a war story is that a fairy tale begins with, "Once upon a time . . ." and ends with " . . . they lived happily ever after," while war stories begin with "There I was . . ." and end with " . . . This is no shit."

The following are perhaps a cross between a war story and a fairy tale. I will not intentionally bend the facts, but find myself in the condition that the former Chief of Staff of the Army, General (Retired) Gordon Sullivan once described as " . . . having ever increasingly clear memories of events that may never have happened." I beg your forgiveness in advance for any such clear memories. They are what I remember.

Fellow Vietnam helicopter pilot Bob Hamilton says the essentials of any war story are that first, the teller of the war story must believe the story; the listener must pretend to believe the story as it is being told, and third, there are usually large quantities of beer close by. I believe the story I am about to tell. There is always plenty of beer in the Flanagan household. All that remains is for the reader to pretend to believe the story as it is being read.

I began this effort to record two or three war stories I didn't want to forget. As the time became available and those areas of my memory were accessed, more stories came to light, and what the heck, I just began to write them down too. Some of the stories are not in strict chronological order. Although I was there and these are my memories of the actions, I was not alone. Each member of the 1st of the 9th is a true hero. The stories are written as I thought about them and remembered them. As I reread them I often added thoughts. I strayed into my personal life, and recorded some of those memories as well. I hope I don't confuse you too much, and I do hope you will enjoy the story anyway.

There I was . . .

Chapter Two

God Bless you.

Before graduating from flight school most folks in the class got orders directly to a unit. These pinpoint assignments allowed the officer to have at least some indication of where he was going to be located for his next tour. Knowing where you were going you could wear that unit patch on your sleeve for the graduation ceremony. Of course these pinpoint assignments were mainly to the large division and separate brigade sized units both stateside and in Vietnam. Judging from the patches on the sleeve fully half of the pilots were going directly to Vietnam. The other half were assigned to stateside posts where units were forming to deploy to Vietnam within the next year.

I didn't receive a pinpoint assignment to any specific unit in Vietnam. My orders assigned me to the replacement detachment of the Military Assistance Command-Vietnam, or MAC-V as it was called. I didn't know why I was one of the few to not have a pinpoint assignment. I had to think this one through. And I came up with the reason for no assignment. You see these other guys were going to the big combat divisions as combat pilots. I knew that there were also a lot of small units of flight detachment size who were VIP (very important people) pilots. That's it! I knew it! I was going to be a VIP pilot—flying the general and his staff, maybe even Bob Hope, or better, the USO girls! I could actually picture myself living in Saigon and ferrying the brass around country.

I knew from all the talk I heard from the Vietnam veteran IPs (instructor pilots) coming through school that the 1st CAV is like a death wish come true. The CAV lived in tents and on air mattresses, and liked it. All they did was fight, fight and fight. The average life span of a helicopter pilot in Vietnam was short, in the CAV it was much shorter. I knew if I went there, I wasn't going to make it back. But a VIP detachment—this is good.

I kept that thought as I prepared to go to Vietnam. I even carried over a portable bar. You know those little briefcases that hold a fifth of liquor, a shot glass, six silver cups, an ice strainer and a silver stirrer. I hand carried one of those things to Vietnam together with my flight helmet, and duffel bag. The bar was bulky all right, but it would be well worth it when I offered MR. Hope an in-flight shot from my private preserve. I could see it plainly.

However halfway through my second full day in Vietnam at the repo depot (replacement center) my classmate Larry Brown yelled at me "Hey Voice, we're going to the CAV." I couldn't believe it. I went to the operation's building to see for myself. I was shocked to see my name there on the list for the 1st Cavalry Division (Airmobile).

Voice is short for "The voice from the back of the room." It is a nickname Al "Fish" De Mailo gave me. I have this strange sense of humor that sees humor in some of the most boring or mundane situations. In flight school, particularly during the pre-flight portion of school, we had to sit in hot classrooms for long stretches of time being lectured on some of the most boring and dry subjects known to man. The instructors were a pretty wild bunch of veteran helicopter pilots whose personalities were weird. In an attempt to keep our attention they would pepper their presentations with jokes and pictures of scantily clad young ladies. Added together this formed a very fertile field for my sense of humor. As the thought would strike me I would share my humor with the class via a series of one-line commentaries. Since I always sat in the back of the room and Fish in the front, Fish named me the "voice from the back of the room." The name stuck even to this day.

The paper order on the operation's bulletin board also identified our classmates who would be going to the Cav and the time we would be shipped out. I went back to my bunk and was almost in despair. I knew for sure, I was not going to make it back home.

Going Up Country Later that day or the next day, consciousness of time has to be one of the first things to leave one when faced with such a hard reality, we were herded onto the floor of an Air Force C-130. I couldn't believe it, we were going up-country like a heard of cattle. Here was a mass of US soldiers with their equipment being jammed, pushed and yelled at by some gung-ho infantry lieutenant trying to get everyone on-board this airplane. There were body parts and baggage covering every available space on the floor of that aircraft. They finally got the doors closed and the ramp up. Thankfully the top part of the clamshell aft ramp was left open during the entire flight for air circulation. Between the heat, the sweaty bodies, and the baggage the smell was pretty bad.

This was unbelievable. After nine months of flight school where we were drilled into safety, safety, safety, here we were sitting on floor with nothing to hold on to. There were no seats, no seat belts, and no straps. There was just flesh to flesh and flesh to floor. I knew it wouldn't be long before I'd be taking that long, last flight into eternity.

We arrived at An Khe the CAV's base camp in the central highlands of Vietnam. We were hot and tired as we arrived in the afternoon at the next repo depot. This one the CAV's own. We were assigned to GP Medium tents with about twenty or so cots in each. The floors of the tent were dirt. The sides of the tent were rolled up halfway to provide some relief from the heat. We quickly set up our cots and learned how to rig up the mesh mosquito net to protect us from the bugs. I stashed my duffel bag, helmet and portable bar under the cot. Since most of the guys were class-mates I felt as though we were back at "Tac X" in flight school. Tac X was a field tactical site where we seniors went for a week of living and operating in the field on realistic tactical missions. Someone came to get us and lead us to the messhall where we ate and got briefed on what was to happen the next day. An Khe was hot and dusty, and we had not yet begun to catch up on the jet lag. Nor had the body gotten adjusted to the heat and dust. Standing around doing nothing added to the overall feeling of fatigue. We all went to bed pretty early. There was nothing to keep us awake even if we wanted to stay up.

In the middle of the night we were awaken by the sounds of loud Whomp! Whomp! Whomp! And the sirens went off blaring loudly into the night. The sirens wail soon mixed with the sounds of Whomp. And there was a distinct noise of people, hidden in the darkness, running around with a sense of urgency. Some voices were heard yelling at someone to "shut that goddamn light out."

Somebody with a CAV patch, steel pot helmet and a rifle came to the tent and said "come on, get down and follow me."

"Oh shit! First night with the CAV and we have a mortar attack?" I thought to myself. Worse. After the mortars, there were sporadic small arms and machine gun firing along what I was to learn was the green line—the concertina wired, barren perim-eter, which surrounded An Khe and acted as a security fence.

The helmeted soldier led us to a ditch and told us to stay put and keep down. This was not an improved ditch. This was just a small natural ditch in the folds of the ground. We didn't have any helmets, guns, or ammunition. We didn't have shit! Didn't know where we were or what to do. I knew then for sure, it's not gonna take very long at all before I take that long trip. And what an insult for an army aviator, to get waxed the first night in the CAV! And by a mortar!

I don't know how long we stayed in the ditch. Sometime later someone woke me up and said we could go back to the tents. We followed the helmeted soldier back through the night to our tent. Finding my bunk I fell into it. Lying there I wondered how often this happened, and whether anyone had breached the perimeter. I also thought about my chances of waking up dead the next morning? I trailed off to sleep with those thoughts. I slept pretty well, until the sun stirred me, and I had to take a leak. Where the hell was I? And where the hell is the latrine?

Someone came and told us what was going to happen that day and where and when we should do whatever. There was no news on what happened last night, and we certainly weren't going to act like newbees and ask all those dumb newbee questions.

Assignment Day The next day was quite organized. They gathered all of us into a big briefing hall. A colonel welcomed us and said that he would first identify each unit of the CAV that needed pilots that day, how many they needed, and a short description of what each unit did. When he completed telling us about each of the units he would go back and, by unit, ask for volunteers. If there weren't enough volunteers to fill the unit needs he would then just assign the remainder.

One by one he described the units. Medevac—flies the D model Huey and shortly the new H model Hueys, etc. Then he came to the First of the Ninth—the First Squadron, Ninth US Cavalry Regiment. Here he said "I need tigers for this one. The 1/9 CAV is the eyes and the ears of the division. They have started every major fight the division has fought in. This is where the action is. I'll need thirteen volunteers for this unit." Since I figured I wasn't gonna make it anyway, why not go out in a blaze of glory and save some other son-of-a-bitch. I made up my mind to volunteer when the time came. I didn't listen much to the rest of the descriptions I knew where I wanted to go. I looked around and tried to figure out who else was gonna go for the gusto.

When the time came the colonel asked for 13 tigers for the 1/9 CAV. More than 13 hands went up, as I recall. He then said "how many are married, raise the other hand." He counted again and told the married the guys, "those with two hands up, thanks, put your hands down. Those with their hands up will be my First of the Ninth tigers."

The procedure followed for each of the units in the 1st Cavalry until the last slot was filled. He didn't ask anyone about being married again. After the list was exhausted the colonel went to one of the 10 or so tables at the front of the room and asked for the 1/9 tigers to come to him. One by one we sat at the table with him, while he took the information—name, serial number, etc. As he finished each of us he stood up, shook hands with the pilot and said "God bless you." Then went on to the next. And so it went.

Curious as to whether he was going to do this for the whole room I lagged behind to observe. As the colonel rose with the last of the thirteen, he shook his hand and said "God bless you." And he turned and the two of them walked towards the door and me. Just then, like clockwork about 8 or so enlisted specialists took their positions at the other tables and began calling out units—227th Aviation Battalion, 229th Aviation Battalion, Medevac, etc. We had been blessed; they were being processed. That Colonel, whoever he was, made it a point to meet and bless each of us single pilots going to the 1/9 CAV. I knew then for sure, I wasn't going to make it home. I hoped it would happen quickly and not wait for my last day of the tour.

Chapter Three

B Troop 1st/ 9th is a long way from Brooklyn

I was born and raised in Brooklyn, New York. The third son, and fifth child of first generation Irish-American parents. My brother Jimmy who was fourth in the birth order died at the age of three, a few days after my first birthday. All four grandparents came from the old country, and both of my parents were born in the US. My father was a laborer working in a civil service position with the New York City Parks Department in Brooklyn's Prospect Park. My mother did not work out of the home. She had her hands full with us, and my father. They tell me my father changed a lot after my brother's death.

We lived in the bottom two floors of my grandmother's 3 story house in the Bush Terminal / Park Slope / Sunset Park area of Brooklyn. The block was a combination of small two family houses and big (run down) apartment houses. On the corner of the block (40th Street) at 4th Avenue was Dewey Junior High School. We would later call it an inner city school. The neighborhood had been mainly Italian and Irish immigrants, with a smattering of Polish, but was being infiltrated, or more precisely being overrun, by an influx of Puerto Ricans.

On the other corner, towards the waterfront and the factories of Bush Terminal, was Third Avenue. Above the avenue was the elevated highway, part of the Gowanus Parkway, which led from the Brooklyn Battery Tunnel east to the Shore Road Parkway. The parkway continued east, paralleling the bay that served as the entrance to New York harbor. You could see the Statue of Liberty as you drove along this route. The parkway continued to the east passing Sheapshead Bay, Coney Island, the Rockaways, and Idlewild (JFK) Airport. It would hook up to the Southern State Parkway that leads to the suburbs—out on the Island. The first generation immigrant Flanagan and Rogan families (Mom and Dad's family) were raised along this route. My uncles from both sides of the family were either cops (New York's Finest) or longshoreman. They were hard workers either way. Most of my aunts worked outside the home. My father and mother were the exception. As I said earlier, he was with the Parks Department, and my Mom stayed home with us.

To say we were poor is an understatement. I've seen worse in my lifetime, but growing up as poor as we were does not make for a great life. I remember going without a hot water heater for years as a kid. And I remember the excitement when we finally got a new one when I was about seven or eight years old. Before that Mom would boil water on the stove in a big teakettle and a big pot, and then carry them upstairs and pour them in the tub. She would add some cold water and then give us baths.

My family occupied the bottom, ground level floor and the second floor of the house. The ground level contained our living room and kitchen, a step down entrance in the front of the house from the "airey way," and a rear entrance through an enclosed rear porch that led to a wooden open porch attached to the rear of the house. The airey way was the fenced in front of the house where the family sat out on a stolen park bench in the summer evenings to pass the time and try to cool off. Under the stairs to the second floor was a stairway that led to the cellar, and the coal fired furnace. The second floor contained the house's only bathroom, and three "railroad" bedrooms. Railroad rooms are rooms that connect from one to the next, as cars of a railroad train. On the top floor my father's mother, Nana lived. She lived alone, though at times members of the family lived there as well.

In my early years of growing up, my Aunt Anna and her son Joey lived with Nana. Joey was like a brother to me. He was a year or so older then me and we used to play, and fight with each other. Joe referred to my father as "Daddy Jim." And my father would always threaten to "kill the pair of yous" if we didn't stop doing what we were doing. Joey and Aunt Anna moved out quickly one day after a very large and loud fight between my father and my aunt. I still don't know what happened. The family was very good at closing down on any information about things that the family didn't want anyone to know about. Very elderly aunts, sisters of Nana as I remember being told, lived on and off upstairs with Nana.

Growing up in that house is still a terrible memory for me. Being the youngest by a lot of years meant that my brother and sisters got to leave home long before I could. My brother Dave got married when I was about 10. My older sister Peggy married when I was twelve or so and moved to California. My other sister, Hannah, stayed in the house the longest with me. Hannah and I got to see the worse of my father. Hannah got married and moved to Staten Island. She and my brother-in-law Bill had me over their house most weekends just to give me a place to be away from the tension and anger. I was an angry kid, and hated everything about my father, and what he did to us.

My sister Peggy and her husband Jerry helped me when after a year or so, they returned from California. They took me along to upstate New York for a week or so when they were looking for a new house. Seems as though every summer they had me up to their place for a week or two to get me away from my father. My brother Dave and my sister-in-law, Noreen, helped by letting Tommy and I baby-sit for them. These diversions helped some, but it wasn't enough to make any real change in the mood in the house, or my feelings towards my father. I am sure I didn't help the situation, but I was angry. Not having a comfortable place to call home, I suppose I sought comfort, acceptance, and happiness outside the house and the family.

From the earliest time I was able, I worked to get some money so I could do things. I was an altar boy who almost lived in church on Saturday and Sunday. This way I could serve at the weddings and split the tips we got. I delivered the weekly Catholic newspaper on a paper route for two cents a paper per weekly delivery. I had about 58 customers along the route. It would take me about three hours to deliver them. The nickel and dime tips most of my customers gave me made it almost worthwhile. Christmas was always a good time to deliver the paper because of the extra tips I received.

During the summers the church's chief maintenance man, would hire us "off the books" to help him fix the church and help with the repairs and maintenance of the school. I learned a lot from that, and should have thanked old Charlie more when I had the chance.

My friends Tommy Jennings, Jimmy Nelson, Steve Mc Farland, and Jimmy Hendren used to work for Charlie too. There was always something for us to do. I don't remember how much we got paid each day. Not much I 'm sure, but a lot more than I would get from home.

Our parish was really big. And with its own elementary school there was always something that needed to get done, and my buddies and me were always available to do the work. Tommy and I were proficient travelers of the subways as we would courier "stuff" for the priests and the nuns. There was always something to rush over to Manhattan or to downtown Brooklyn for the parish. Since we were so young they always sent two of us. Sometimes instead of giving us carfare money, they would "lend" us bus and subway passes so we could ride the subways and buses for free. I guess we were breaking the law, but we only got stopped once in Manhattan and were able to talk our way out of it.

I don't really know if my parents were aware of all the time we spent out of school. All this and we were still in grade school. Most of the time in grade school I had thought I would go into the priesthood. I saw how the priests had it made. Monsignor Nolan, Father Calderwood, Father Cummings, Father Collins, Father Brown, Father "Rod" Rodriquez, Father Cutler, they were the priests at Saint Michael's that I remember most. They had cars, had a maid, had a cook, and lived in the rectory for free. They seemed really happy, and did lots of stuff that sounded like fun. Many of them went on cruises for vacations and they always seemed to have neat cars, and for the most part are happy guys. There was the religious stuff too, that seemed okay. At least I wouldn't go to hell, I thought. I kept this orientation for the priesthood until midway in my freshman year.

Of all of the priests, Father Rod had the most effect on my friends and me. He taught us so many things about the Church, about ourselves, about him, and about life in general. He took us to so many restaurants and taught us the better side of life. I first had clams and oysters with Rod. He was a good man, a super priest, and a great friend.

I graduated from grammar school and received a scholarship to one of the Diocesan high schools run by the Irish Christian Brothers. I went to Saint Augustine High School, and enjoyed it for the first half of my freshman year. At the end of the first year however, I knew I didn't want to come back and I asked my parents to be transferred to a public school. My parents wouldn't let me. I went to summer school that year and had a great time at Erasmus Hall High School a public school. The coed classes were a refreshing change from the male only, suit and tie student body at Saint Augustine's. (Gabe Kaplin, of the "Welcome Back Kotter" TV went to Erasmus Hall High School.)

Knowing the rules of the school and still committed to getting away from the Irish Christian Brothers, I didn't do any work the first half of my sophomore year, and was thrown out for poor grades. My Mom and I ran into Tommy and his Mom the same day in the admissions office of the public school—John Jay High

School. The mothers were not very happy. Tom and I were pretty excited to be there. We had talked about the possibility of getting back together in the same school. Now we were together again. Tom and I took the battery of placement tests necessary to assign us to the right class level. The teacher / counselor, an older Jewish teacher, administering and grading the tests was amazed at how smart we both were. She acted as if she hadn't seen anyone with a brain in a very long time. She fussed and fussed over us, and gave us more and more tests. She was impressed. After the first few days in the new school we understood why; there were a lot of loggerheads in that school. Some of these folks had been left back so often they could vote in their sophomore year. In any case, she told me I had an aptitude for law and Tommy for teaching, and we should definitely plan on going to a good college.

"Yeah" I thought to myself, "go to college?" My family couldn't afford to send me to Catholic High School with more than one suit for the entire year, how could they afford to send me to college? Besides what was I gonna be when I grew up? A cop like the rest of the family? Not that there is anything wrong with being a cop, but you didn't need a college degree to be one. The future was not very bright at all. But for now, at least Tommy and I were together in school again. We seemed to be doing everything together.

John Jay High School was fun. It used to be called Manual Training High School. When the book and the movie *Blackboard Jungle* told the story of the school its name was Manual Training High School. I guess the name was changed to protect the guilty. In any case, we sort of did what we wanted to do at John Jay. Tommy and I had a lot of classes together. We also cut a lot of classes together. We also took care of each other as we each worked as teachers' aides. Our duties included maintaining the official attendance books and checking homework assignments. There was power in these jobs. We could give credit to our friends and even change some grades to help them through some of the classes. We also had access to the student registration cards that were like gold. Our school had three lunch periods each day to handle the large student body. The cafeterias couldn't handle all the students so some students and all seniors were allowed to leave the school for lunch. Of course your registration card had to show that you were eligible to leave for that lunch period. We always had at least three registration cards so we could leave anytime we wanted.

Tom and I also used some street logic on a couple of teachers to absent ourselves from class. One semester we had a second year French class as our last period. We were always cutting up and being really disruptive in this class. One Monday we returned after having cut the entire week before. We weren't in the class more than ten minutes when the teacher said "Flanagan, Jennings, you two were so good last week, why are you acting up so early this week?" Tom and I knew then that attendance was voluntary in this class. We cut his class often to shoot pool before going to work. Even with cutting so much we were still able to pass the NYS Regents examination.

Tom, Denis, Jim Hendren and I worked in the kitchen of a local hospital—The Lutheran Medical Center. It stood on the corner of 4th Avenue and 45th Street. Tom's mom worked there for years and helped get us the jobs. We worked there for the first two years of high school. When there was a change in the contractors who ran the kitchen, Tommy and I quit. We made a lot of the same decisions.

We began dating girls together. Our girlfriends were best friends too. Linda was only twelve years old when we first began dating. My first recall of the start of the attraction was passing by this house on 4th Avenue and some girls smiling at us. Tommy and I realized there was something going on so we passed by again and this time when they smiled we stopped and began to talk to them. Tom and I were about a year or so older than them. Before we knew it we were hanging around with them and there "single" girlfriends all of the time. Tom and Jim alternatively dated Gay Ann and Maryanna. We dated these girls throughout our high school years. Our group included Ann Marie, Sandra, Anna, Kathy, Joanne, Peter, John and Tom Pakruda. Tom and Maryanna, and, Pete and Anna ended up married to each other. We group dated a lot. And whether we were walking along Fifth Avenue window shopping, hanging out at the beach at Coney Island, or going to De Barrow's Ice Cream Parlor (DeeBee's) after church, we were mostly in a group. Tom and I were always in the middle of four to six girls who were friends. We also spent a lot of time at Linda's. In the early evenings when the weather allowed, we mostly sat on her stoop as her Mom and Dad (Rose and John) sat in the folding beach chairs and Linda's younger sisters pestered us. Rose and John became "Mom" and "Pop" to all of us. I think of them as my second parents. I learned a lot of things from talking and hanging around them. They were a close, loving family.

After quitting the hospital kitchen job I went job hunting. Linda's dad worked as a buyer or purchasing agent for the Great Atlantic and Pacific Tea Company. The factory was located in the Bush Terminal buildings a few blocks from where I lived. He told me to apply there and let him know when I going to fill out the application. I went down the next day. As I was filling out the application Pop dropped by and introduced me to the person taking the application. Needless to say I got the job. I didn't realize it but I had applied for a fulltime job working 3:30 PM to midnight shift. This meant I would get home from school at 2:45PM, eat a snack, and then walk to work. I would take my supper in a brown bag. The factory was amazing. They made pasta, spaghetti, candy and so many other things there. I was just a laborer. I swept the floors. One night I operated a pallet jack moving pallets of boxed noodles. Another night I was in charge of operating a machine that pulverized little curls of pasta that were left over in the preparation process. The curls were pulverized back into fine granules and mixed back into the mix. The factory was a big operation. I learned a lot about working there. Mostly that I really didn't want to do this for the rest of my life. Honest and honorable work, yes; but I thought I would go crazy being stuck in a factory. The machines were neat and the people were entertaining, but not what I wanted to do. In any case the experience was wild. The money was really very good. But working full time and going to school got old, real fast. There wasn't much time left in the day when you work the 3:30 to midnight shift and have to be up for school at 6 AM the next day. As luck would have it, one of the priests called the local bank where they did business and found out they were looking for a rack clerk. I applied and was hired. This time I made sure I was getting a part time job.

After four and a half years I finally graduated from high school with a Regent's Academic Diploma in January 1965. I received a New York State Regents Scholarship to help with college, but couldn't afford to go full-time. I started to go to night school in Manhattan. I remember vividly going with my mother to the loan officer at the bank I worked to apply for a $100 loan to pay for the remainder of the tuition not covered by the scholarship.

I immediately went to work full-time at that bank after graduation. The bank sent me to school to train as a teller. I was the youngest teller in the CitiBank chain when I graduated from teller training school. I didn't know what I wanted to do with my life. The bank job and night school kept me pretty busy.

Linda moved to Philadelphia around the time I graduated. I was heartbroken. We had done so much together and really had grown up together. But her dad's factory was closing and the job in Philadelphia presented an attractive offer. We stayed in touch as best we could. She invited me to her prom and I took the bus to Philly and stayed at her house. Time and distance played its part and we finally broke up in late summer. I had a rough time over it for a good while.

About August 1965 I realized I wasn't getting anyplace fast. My buddies and I were all arriving at the same place at the same time, and together realized we needed to do something with our lives. The certainty of the draft increased as the war in Vietnam continued to grow. Many of my co-workers of draft age were taking the safe tracks and getting into the overcrowded National Guard and Reserve units. I had the opportunity to do this as well. (My brother knew a guy in a reserve component Green Beret unit on Staten Island I could get into. Yeah right? Me? Afraid of heights, and he wants me to jump from an airplane? Sure. And this is my brother that till this day won't get on an airplane?) Linda had moved away and so that was over I was sure. I knew I had to do something. I knew the time had come for a big change.

I had taken a number of civil service tests as part of one class I took in high school. We took practice tests—post office, clerks test, police, fire—during the class and practiced filling out applications. On our own time we could take the test for real, and I did. I passed them all with pretty good scores. I was called for the police test but had difficulty with the physical part of the exam. I would have to work on my pull-ups and push-ups. And Dave wanted me to be a Special Forces Green Beret?

My buddies and I had visited all the recruiters and heard their sales pitch. "Before you get drafted, we can give you a choice," they all said. Always partial to the color blue, and in love with flying, I was most interested in the Air Force. But that meant an enlistment of 4 years and they didn't really guarantee which job you were going to get. And you couldn't fly unless you were an officer, and for that you had to have a college degree. The Air Force wasn't going to be my choice.

The Marines? Well there were the Marines. But I didn't like PT and running and stuff like that. (Never did, still don't.) Besides other friends I had, and older guys I knew, were different when they came back from Marine boot camp. I thought (and still do) that Marines were brainwashed. Besides if I wanted to be tough, I could always see Dave's friend in Special Forces and not risk going to Vietnam.

The Navy held no attraction for me at all. I couldn't fathom being on a ship for months at a time and no girls around. What do you do on a ship all day? Now I know; they work all day and night on a rotation basis. I'll trade the Navy's clean sheets every night my uncles always talked about for the company of a young lady every now and then, anytime.

I went to the Army recruiter but all he would talk about was a four-year enlistment. I knew how long four years was, I just graduated from high school and it's a long time. (Okay, it took me four and half years.) I can still appreciate the length of four years versus two years if you were drafted.

Jimmy McKee broke up with his girlfriend Maureen. She lived in Manhattan and they had been dating for a while. Jimmy McKee decided to join the Marines. Tom Jennings and Jimmy Hendren enlisted in the Air Force. Tom became a jet engine mechanic, and Jimmy served as a crew chief on a B52. And me?

What I did was push my draft date up by volunteering for the draft. This way I knew I was going to go soon, but that it would be for only two years. As it turned out I received my draft notice the same morning I was selected for training as the head teller at the Montague Street branch in downtown Brooklyn. I was to be First National City Bank's youngest head teller, they told me. My Mom called me at the bank that morning and told me I had received mail from the Selective Service Board. She was almost in tears and spoke with a tremble in her voice. I told her to open it and read it. It said something like:

Greetings:

Your friends and neighbors have selected you to defend our Country. Meet them at 0500 hours, Thursday morning, 3 February 1966, their place—Whitehall Street, New York.

Sincerely,
    Your Selective Service Board

The letter had a subway token scotch taped across the letter-head. I told my branch manager that I had been drafted and that I would probably have to take a military leave of absence. The next day I told him when my last day would be. Before I left for the Army, I took a Greyhound bus up to Burlington, Vermont to see my sister Peggy and her family for a few days. I had plenty of time to think about what was happening on that bus ride to Burlington Vermont and back.

A couple of days before I left for Basic Training my Aunt Anna Anderson (my Mom's sister, who worked at Albany Cycle, a toy store in Brooklyn) gave me a GI JOE action figure with a crisp new twenty dollar bill in his right hand. In the box was an official GI Joe ID Card and application for the GI Joe Fan Club, which entitled me to monthly newsletters. I sent the application in and received correspondence from my comrade in arms throughout basic training and flight school. The letters stopped when I went to Vietnam. I left the action figure with my Mom. My nephews would play with him while I was gone. I still have him; he's probably worth more today than the twenty dollars he had in his hand when I got him.

Jimmy McKee was the first to go. He went to the Marines. He was the shortest in height of our group. He was also in the best physical shape. It figured for him to go to the Marines. We all went out the night before he left and had a great time. We all stayed at his house that night and gave him a great send off the next morning.

I went next. We went out the night before and partied, then slept over my house and had a good time. Tommy rode the taxi-cab to Whitehall Street with me the next morning—February 3rd, 1966. Tom went next. Jimmy Hendren continued the tradition and stayed with Tom the night before. It is a shame that I couldn't be with Tom and Jim and give them the same send off they gave me. It's a shame that Jim Hendren didn't have a proper send off. Thank God we all survived our tours of service with the military during this, the height of the Vietnam War. Amazingly, of the four of us, I was the only one who stayed on for more than one hitch. I stayed for twenty years. I didn't mean to, it just happened that way.

13's My Lucky Number The Induction Station at Whitehall Street in Lower Manhattan serviced the needs of all the services and all the components. Regardless, Army, Navy, draftee, enlistee, active or reserve component, Whitehall Street did it all. I didn't know this until that 3 February 1966. Another thing I didn't know about. If the Marines didn't get all the "few good men" they needed, they drafted them from the draftees reporting for induction at Whitehall Street.

Now I must admit that before they drafted their fill, they encouraged and asked for volunteers to join the Marines. It surprised me that not only were they drafting Marines, but that some people were actually volunteering for it. This day they didn't get enough volunteers, despite all of their Marine logic and reasoning they used to convince guys to volunteer. It finally came time for them to fill out the roster for induction into and shipment to the United States Marine Corps.

We were standing on line in some hallway in our shorts and socks with our possessions in a cloth bag tied around our necks, when two marines with stripes all over the place began counting from the front of the line. "One..two..three.." he counted loudly until he reached the guy in front of me. The marine sergeant still touching the guy's shoulder announced "Twelve." He went on, "You twelve men, take two steps forward." Then, "Congratulations you have been selected to become United States Marines. Move out!" And they disappeared as they made the turn at the end of the hallway.

Thirteen. I was number thirteen.

At twelve you're a Marine; at thirteen you were Army.

Thank God! This has got to be my lucky number from here on in, for the rest of my life. I don't know what I would have done if I had been one of the twelve. I seriously believe I would have been in Canada.

I asked my brother Dave to do the first edit of this book. He did a great job of it too. When he came to this part he told me that my father's lucky number was also 13. He went on to say that my father had been a bricklayer when he was younger and that one day while he was laying bricks for a big building from a scaffold on the thirteenth floor the scaffold gave way. He was able to hold on to the ropes until they rescued him. Unfortunately the guy with him fell to his death.

Chapter Four

Reception Station

Those of us who had passed all of the tests and finished processing were directed into a room where we were lined up in rows according to alphabetical order. We stood with our toes touching a white line on the floor. We were instructed to raise our right hands and when our first and last names were called we were to take one step forward give our middle name and, when everyone had been called forward we were to repeat the oath of enlistment. So what if you didn't have a middle name? When they called your first and last names you would step forward and say "no middle name." The Army had everything covered.

A lot of thoughts went through my mind as I stood there for the first time and took the oath. Is this what I really wanted to do? Would this be the beginning of the end for me? Mostly though there were thoughts about, what the hell have you gotten yourself in for now Flanagan? It was too late now to second guess my decision.

"Flanagan, John" the sergeant barked.

"Edward" I said, and took one step forward.

After being sworn in we were divided into groups according to which reception station and military base we were going to. I stood in the group going to Fort Jackson, South Carolina.

We left Whitehall Street late that afternoon and went to Grand Central Station where we boarded a train for Washington DC, enroute to Fort Jackson, South Carolina. Waiting at the station we saw two MPs escorting a third soldier who was in handcuffs. I thought to myself, "could that be me in a few weeks?" I wonder what he did? Was it something really bad? Or was it just something really little. We all had heard stories of the services being harsh on some pretty petty things. We never did find out what he did.

We arrived in the Washington DC train station at about 11:30 that night. We changed trains to one with sleeper cars. On the boarding platform that night as we changed trains there were a few flag draped caskets on baggage carts obviously awaiting transportation to Arlington. I gave some very serious thoughts about what I had gotten myself into.

The sleeper car didn't much relieve the anxiety either. I had the top bunk. Rich Waldron, a guy from Long Island, who became my first Army buddy, took the lower bunk. The top bunk was pretty cramped. And the ceiling curved over the top of me seemingly inches over my face. The privacy curtain clung close to my side and blocked out almost all of the light from the dimmed night lights in the sleeper car. The thought struck me that this is very similar to the view the guys under the flags were experiencing back there on the railroad platform.

The Fort Jackson reception station was overcrowded when we got there. The old World War II wooden barracks were packed. So much so they had added a tent city to the reception station. Row upon row of GP (General Purpose) medium tents, each with two coal burning stovepipes sticking out the top of the tents. The weather was cold, windy and wet. The place was pretty muddy, too. I was lucky though and got into one of the barracks. The folks that had been there in the morning had shipped out to basic training. We were assigned to bunk in the barracks. Later, some soldier came in and taught us how to make our bunks and told us where to put the stuff we came with. We received a bunch of briefings that seemed to drone on for eternity. Funny thing, the more they briefed us the less we knew, and the more confused we all became. Much of the confusion came from the language they were using. I could tell they were speaking English. But the English was horrible! They were speaking southern English. Spoken so slow, and drawn out, and peppered with y'alls and incorrect verbs. Their English was terrible. I remember wondering if you had to be a southerner and ignorant to be a sergeant in the Army.

The next day we were awakened in what seemed to be the middle of the night. Lights shot on. People (Sergeants and corporals, we later learned they were called cadre) started screaming about getting up, get shaved, get dressed, make your bunk and fall outside for breakfast. We did the best we could I guess, but not fast enough for the cadre. We fell out of the barracks into the darkness and cold of the morning. There was more screaming at all of us. Then the sergeants would get in somebody's face and really scream at him, calling him every name in the book. I was not having any fun at all. My only comfort was that I could imagine what those twelve guys in front of me at Whitehall Street were going through at Paris Island, at that very minute.

They marched us in a big gaggle in the early morning darkness down the road and across the post it seemed. Finally we arrived at the mess hall where we had to wait outside, while the cadre jumped in your face and screamed at you.

Going through the chow line for my first breakfast was something else as well. You just held your tray up in front of you and walked shoulder to shoulder, sidestepping with the next guy and the KPs (kitchen police, as servers and daily kitchen helpers were referred) just plopped stuff on your tray. When you got to the end you went and sat down at these big picnic kind of tables with individual round seats attached. The cadre continued to yell and scream. You had to stand behind a place at the table and wait until all the places were taken before you were allowed to sit down and eat.

Going through the breakfast line one KP plopped some white stuff with a mound of melted butter in the middle on my metal tray. It looked like some sort of mashed potatoes with butter in the valley on top. Next came the eggs, the bacon and toast.

I am a mashed potato person, and even though I thought it strange to see them on a breakfast plate I dug deeply into them right off. I put a big, really big spoonful in my mouth. As soon as I got them into my mouth I knew something was wrong. These weren't mashed potatoes! These things were gritty, and tasteless. I turned my head away from the table as I thought I was going to throw up! I finally swallowed what I had in my mouth and turned back around. While my head was turned some son of a bitch had stolen a slice of my toast. I began to yell, but one of the cadre was close by yelling at everyone not to talk or speak. "Man. I am not liking this place at all," I told myself. And I asked, "what the hell was that white shit with the butter on it?" I learned later that grits is the staple of the south and I had just had my first taste of it. I have tried them a few times over the years but have not been able to acquire the taste for them at all.

The days in the Reception Station were very long days. They were filled with in-processing and uniform fitting and issue and endless testing. They would bring us in to these buildings which were filled with wood fashioned into desk-like tables. The individual places or desks were defined by vertical wood partitions rising from the desktop to above head level. This to prevent you from cheating from your neighbors' paper. Based on what I saw and learned about my mostly southern comrades I had met in the Army so far, I would never ever even think about copying their answers. These guys didn't only talk slow . . . they did everything slow.

Endless testing in poorly lit rooms, on uncomfortable chairs, after having been kept up late and woken up early was the norm. And when you weren't inside getting tested, you were outside trying to learn how to march. They called it "dismounted drill."

If not for the smoke breaks—"smoke'm if you got 'em"—when you were allowed to sit down, you'd die from the fatigue.

A few days into the reception station and after the tests were scored we were brought to a building. We were told we would be interviewed, and based on the needs of the service, our scores on the tests, and our desires, we would be assigned for training in one of the Army's many military occupational specialties (MOS). When my turn came I picked up my personnel folder containing my test scores, and went to the cubicle where the next clerk was.

I could see the others in front of me weren't spending a lot of time discussing their choices. In fact, it looked as though they were spending less than a minute with the counselor. So when my counselor asked curtly "What do you want to do in the Army?"

I replied " I want to fly a f*cking helicopter."

The clerk stopped writing something on my file, looked at my test scores quickly, and said "Go out that door and go to building such'n'such." He thrust my file at me and I went out the door.

The rest of the "serial"—that's what they called us as we were being processed—stayed behind. "Serials." I don't know what that means even till today. In fact, I hadn't thought of that word until just now. Serials. Huh?

In any case the rest of the serial was standing in a loose formation right outside the door. I was told to go to this other building across the street. So I bypassed them and went towards this other building. There was something different about this building than all the rest of the buildings. Although a World War II building like the rest, this building was painted red, white, and blue.

The Draftee's Deal of a Lifetime.

I entered and was greeted by a sergeant in dress greens with stripes that seemed to begin at his shoes and extend upwards to his shoulders. He was smiling, grabbed my hand and shook it and introduced himself. Man this is different.

I told him what I knew. I had been sent here after I said I wanted to fly. The sergeant pointed me towards a table with coffee, Kool-Aid and doughnuts on it. He said "Help yourself soldier," as he looked over my scores. He told me to sit down in an area where there were about twenty or thirty chairs, and to relax. I picked a seat close to the window. I sat there eating my doughnuts and, alternately drinking coffee and Kool-Aid, and looking out the window at the rest of the serial. As I watched and waited, a number of other guys came from the classification building to the red, white and blue building. One of them was Rich Waldron.

We were gathered together and put in another room that looked more like a classroom where we were given two tests: the military Flight Aptitude Screening Test (FAST) and the officer candidate school (OCS) qualification test. I passed both of them. We were briefed on the schools and the various deals and options open to us.

If we got a certain score on the FAST we would be eligible to apply for flight school after we completed basic combat and advanced individual training (BCT and AIT). If however, we attained a certain score, many points above the basic qualification score, I think around 20 or 25 points higher, we would be offered a direct appointment to the school. This meant we would only have to complete basic training (8 weeks) and then go to flight school. Since flight school was nine months long, we could be Warrant Officers within a year.

Once we got to flight school we would be advanced to the pay grade of E-5; and, once we completed our pre-flight training, which would last about one month, we would begin drawing enlisted flight pay each month. $55 dollars flight pay was nothing to sneeze at when a private's pay was set at about $87 a month at the time. This was a good deal. In just a couple of months I could be drawing a sergeant's pay plus flight pay. But wait there has got to be a catch. And there was.

Here's the deal. In order to accept this direct appointment

you had to first go RA (Regular Army). But, unlike the regular army deal the recruiter in Brooklyn offered the enlistment would be for only two years from the date that I accepted the deal. Okay that meant that if I signed up today I would have to spend 2 years and 6 days total, instead of just two years. No problem, I thought.

Next upon graduating from flight school and receiving a warrant I would be obligated for two years from the date I graduated. Okay, so if I really graduate, I owe them two years, that would make a total of 3 years and 6 days. Okay, but what if I don't graduate? If I didn't graduate, or refused to accept the warrant after completing the entire program, I would revert back to the regular army and have to complete the remainder of my two-year enlistment.

The kid from Brooklyn figured it this way: I go RA and go through flight school quitting on the last day. That should eat up about 11 months of my 24-month obligation. I also figured it would take the Army a month or so to figure out what they wanted to do with me so, I would have less than 12 months remaining. I get one-month leave every year, so that brings it up to 14 months eaten up. Since the tour in Vietnam was for one year, I figured they didn't have enough time to send me there. So I would spend two years and 6 days in the Army, have all the training as a pilot, good bucks for the first year, and I wouldn't have to go to Vietnam. That's the deal I wanted.

But wait, what's this OCS stuff? I was told I passed Officer Candidate School test, too. The OCS deal was to go to basic and advanced infantry training and then go to OCS. After graduating from OCS as an infantry second lieutenant, I could then apply for flight school.

Rich Waldron was faced with the same decision. He had been through a couple of years of ROTC at the University of Dayton, and knew the difference between a lieutenant and a warrant officer and tried to explain it to me. Together we thought our options through, neither of us wanting to be a light weapons infantryman in Vietnam.

As it turned out, I could get a similar deal through OCS as warrant officer school, but you get an obligation of two years after graduating from OCS plus another year after flight school. That's four years, and no guarantee of flight school. Also you didn't get flight pay while in OCS so there was a loss of incentive there. For OCS you needed to only score a 112 on the general aptitude score, but for flight school you needed a 115. (Or something closely approximately those scores.) Weighing all the factors Rich and I went with the first deal and signed up for the Warrant Officer Rotary Wing Aviation Course (WORWAC).

On February 9th, 1966, I was honorably discharged as a Private in the Army of the United States (AUS) and immediately sworn in as Private in the Regular Army (RA). My service number prefix changed from US to RA. The deal was sealed, and I was on my way to flight school instead of Vietnam.

WORWAC candidates took their basic training at Fort Polk Louisiana, so those of us who signed up for the program became "holdovers" in the reception station when the rest of the company shipped out to basic training. They shipped out in the morning and a new bunch of serials came in that afternoon. Funny thing, since we had uniforms, we were soldiers to these new guys, and they were recruits. Because of our new status, we could now go to the snack bar at night where we could get beer and pizza and play the pinball machine.

Even though I was in the Army for just a few short days I learned an important lesson. I found out who the smartest person in world was regardless of the situation. Who is this person, you ask? Simple, it's the person sitting next to you. Here we were all brand new folks in a new situation and told to go sit on the bus. Not knowing where you were going, what do you do? You ask the guy sitting next to you. Why? Because he must be smarter than you.

As holdovers we did have to pull duty however. We pulled

CQ runner. The CQ, or charge of quarters was the commander's representative during the evening hours. The CQ runner, was just that, he ran the errands for the CQ. If someone needed Smith, the CQ runner would run over and find Smith. One evening the weather got pretty bad and the CQ told me to go to the tent area and make sure the recruits tighten up their tents so they wouldn't blow down. Huh? Me? Show them how to keep the tent from blowing down in the storm? Are you kidding, I've never been in a tent? My brother Dave, he was a Boy Scout; he could probably help, but me? Well we went down to the tent city and I guess we did okay. The "we" included a guy from Virginia Beach by the name of Phil Flanagan—no relation, but he was going to flight school too. Not all of the tents came down, and only one suffered some fire damage as I recall, when the canvas hit one of the stoves on the way down.

We were also in charge of marching the serials back and forth to the messhall. I guess since we knew a little more than the guys with no uniforms, we were the "best qualified." I remember one morning coming back from breakfast Phil Flanagan was calling cadence and marching the group when something distracted him at the back of the formation. He almost had the front of the formation march off a steep incline. I had trouble holding back my laughter, seeing how funny Phil looked as he was trying to regain his composure.

I wouldn't call it homesick, but I felt a lot of loneliness. I called my Mom a couple of times just to hear her voice. I called Linda to tell her I was in the army and going to flight school. I had hoped I could impress her. I didn't. Oh well, the army was keeping me pretty busy, and probably would for the next two years. I found out that when you are busy you don't have much time to feel lonely.

Basic Training—Fort Polk, Louisiana February 1966 When the time came, we were flown via commercial air from Fort Jackson, South Carolina to Fort Polk, Louisiana. I had flown a couple of times before beginning when I was about 11 or 12 years old. These were on American Airlines from New York City's La Guardia airport to Boston's Logan Field. American flew some good two engine tricycle gear aircraft. The airlines we flew on to Fort Polk were the old tail dragging DC-3s. You remember seeing them in all the old World War II pictures with parachutists coming out the side doors. Man, that was some trip. When you entered the plane through the back door you had to bend forward so you wouldn't knock your head on the ceiling. And then you had to walk this way up the about 30-degree incline to get to your seat. Let me tell you, I thought over this decision of mine to go to flight school a number of times during that flight. This was some pretty scary flying.

We were sent to Delta Company, 1st Battalion, 1st Training Brigade. We arrived during cycle break and became "snowbirds." Snow birds were students who showed up for training before the training cycle was scheduled to begin. All of the snowbirds were like Rich and I, they had signed up for the WORWAC program too. In addition to Rich Waldron, there was Phil Flanagan, Russ Doersam, Wiley Hazelwood, Doug Sparks, Tony Marchovich, Al Subotky, and Jim Rucker. Surprisingly, we all made it through BCT. (And flight school, too!)

We pulled detail every day. The company was doing some local renovation of barracks. We removed built-in wardrobes so the new metal wall lockers could be brought in. Being snowbirds gave us a head start on the rest of the company who was being formed in the Fort Polk reception station. We got to know most of the drill sergeants and company cadre.

Being known by the cadre was a double-edged sword. One day in formation as the drill sergeant was drilling us on our general orders he came up to me. I snapped to attention as he addressed me.

" Flanagan, do you need to know you general orders to fly them helicopters?" he barked.

"Yes Drill Sergeant!" I replied screaming at the top of my lungs.

"Why do you say that Private Flanagan?" he asked loudly with a quizzical look on his face.

"Because if I don't learn my general orders I will never get out of basic training, Drill Sergeant!" I yelled back.

"You're goddamn right, Flanagan" he said trying to control a big laugh and moved on to the next trainee.

Fort Polk had a pretty big hospital complex on it. An endless number of one story wooden world war two buildings connected together by covered walkways, appeared to be some representation of a spider's web laid flat on the ground. The Polk Hospital had flight surgeons assigned to give all the Class I flight physicals. Flight surgeons were medical doctors who had completed a specialized training course studying the physiology of aviation. In order to start flight school you needed to pass a Class I flight physical. One requirement was for 20/20 uncorrected vision in both eyes. After entering school you needed to only pass a Class II physical. In the class II, glasses were allowed, so long as your vision could be corrected to 20/20, and your night vision stayed okay. But this was a Class I Flight Physical we had to pass.

A few weeks into our basic training cycle, the guys in my company who had been selected for flight training, were sent over to take our flight physicals. This was some physical. I had never been prodded or poked so much as this one. I didn't much care, still don't, for the digital rectal, but they did that too. They also did a glaucoma test by first dilating your eyes as you lay on a table, and then as you stared at a mark on the ceiling they placed a weight on each eye to check the pressure. After the physical, we were held at the hospital while the results were checked.

My name was called and I was sent back to the eye examination area. A doctor came in and checked my eyes again and made me do the eye test over. He told me that I had a slight stigmatism that made one eye be 20/25. Thus, he was sorry to tell me, I didn't qualify for the flight program.

"This can't be happening," I told myself.

The "plan" was out the window now. And North Fort Polk was named "Tiger Country" and boasted having its own Vietnam Village where the AIT for light weapons infantrymen could hone their skills before shipping out to Vietnam as their first assignment.

"Oh shit! There has got to be a way," I told myself. I gotta think quickly!

Before coming in the army, I had read a number of books and seen all the old war movies about flying and stories about the guys going through flight school in WWII and Korea. I asked the doctor if I could do anything to strengthen my eyes. Perhaps I could do some pencil focusing drills to exercise and strengthen my eye muscles. I think I had seen this done by Ronald Reagan in one of the war flicks.

The doctor looked at me with a puzzled look when I asked him this. He asked me if I knew that if I graduated from flight school I was heading to "straight to Vietnam?"

"Yes sir." I replied.

He asked if I knew the life expectancy of a helicopter pilot was about three months in Vietnam?

"I don't care, I want to fly helicopters." I said.

He picked up my physical paperwork and shaking his head said 'If you want to die that bad, who am I to stand in your way." He changed my test scores to read 20/20 in both eyes, handed me my physical and said "Good luck." Shaking his head back and forth as he left the room.

I was always afraid to tell that story for fear the Army would come back and take my wings (and pay!) away from me. I don't know who that young Army Captain Doctor was, but I would love to thank him and tell him some of the good things I was able to do because he let me go to flight school.

It's funny, but that is the only flight physical where I scored less than 20/20 until 1975, some 9 years later, when I began to use reading glasses. Of course that was only the beginning. Next came glasses fulltime, then bifocals.

Mornings at Fort Polk The thing that sticks in my memory the most is the smell of the morning in basic combat training at Fort Polk, Louisiana in the winter. Cold—you can see you breath in the dark, poorly lit area between the barracks. The heavy smell and soot of the coal burning furnaces that heated each of the barracks built for temporary use during WWII, mixed with the smell of good strong army coffee and the smell of bacon cooking. Man that was a smell to behold. Till this day whenever I smell coal burning in the morning my mind goes back to those early mornings at Fort Polk.

Holdovers Again Basic training is basic training. If you heard one story about it ever, you have heard them all. Basic combat training was conducted at South Fort Polk. North Fort Polk was used for advanced individual training. Fort Polk's AIT was for light infantry. They referred to North Fort Polk as Tiger Land. In Tiger Land the grunts were trained and prepared to go to Vietnam. On our graduation day we graduated alongside a battalion of infantry AIT soldiers, the majority of which were on orders to Vietnam, and would be in country within two weeks

We graduated from basic training and were held over again. This time because we had a "no earlier than" reporting date at The Primary Helicopter Flight Training School at Fort Wolters, Texas. This wasn't a problem at all. It fit into the plan real well. It meant that our graduation date would be delayed a few more days, thus shortening the time available for them to send me to Vietnam after I quit the day before graduation.

As holdovers we pulled detail. I drew KP most of the days. KP wasn't too bad. You were inside all day and relatively comfortable. There was always chocolate milk available to drink. I always favored the job of side sink man. This is the guy who got the trays and silverware from the troops after each has dumped any remaining chow into the separated trash—edible, inedible. My job was to operate the dishwasher machine, just like in the kitchen at the Lutheran Medical Center where I worked with Tom, Jim and Denis.

Finally the day came when we could sign out of the company and Fort Polk and head home for leave. We were able to sign out at midnight and get on our way. We split a cab to the airport. Cramped in the back seat of the cab overloaded with our duffel bags the ride was rough throughout the long trip. I think we went to the New Orleans airport, but I could be mistaken. I remember really being exhausted after what was the roughest cab ride I had ever experienced.

At the airport we saw for the first time a Warrant Officer Candidate. He was waiting for a flight back to Fort Wolters. He looked sharp in his khaki uniform with the international orange felt background on his highly polished WOC brass on his collar. On his overseas cap he wore his brass atop a circular plastic disk colored to indicate the WOC company he was assigned. I don't recall which company he was in. For us it would be a blue disk signifying we were members of the 3rd WOC Company. A couple of the guys went over and talked to him. I stayed back. I guess I felt it better not to know anything, than to learn about something I might regret later.

I don't remember too much about leave. I felt good seeing my Mom and visiting with the family again. The neighborhood was pretty boring since most of my buddies were still away in training. I didn't really have girlfriend either. Though I did go out several times with some of the girls I went to school with and had some fun. I guess I was still unsure of what I wanted to be when I grew up. Looking back I realize I was only 19 years old and the uncertainty was probably appropriate. Of course now at 55 years old I still don't know what I really want to be.

This reminds me of the story of the father taking his son to airport where they meet an Army helicopter pilot who lets them get in the helicopter. Afterwards as they are standing there watching the helicopter take off, the son looks at his Dad and says, "When I grow up I want to be a helicopter pilot." The dad looks back and says "Sorry son, you can't do both."

Chapter Five

Fort Wolters

We met in Dayton Ohio. We, meaning about six of the guys who had gone through the reception station and basic training together. Rich and I flew in from New York and stayed with his frat brothers at the University of Dayton. Russ Doersam drove in and picked us up. Jim Rucker or Al Subotky may have come with us as well. I don't remember now for sure. Perhaps they did and we took two cars. We drove from Dayton, Ohio to Mineral Wells Texas. Texas is a lot further away than I thought. All the way there all we talked about was what we each thought would happen in flight school, and what it really would be like to fly. We spent one night in a motel in Texarkana. The next day we continued to on to our destiny.

We changed into our uniforms at a gas station in Fort Worth because our orders directed we should report in that way. We drove the next 30 miles through Weatherford and Garner Texas in a more subdued manner until we turned into the gates of Fort Wolters.

The entrance to Fort Wolters had a helicopter on each of the pedestals positioned on cither side of the main gate. On one side was the Bell OH-13 and on the other, the Hiller OH-23. The post was beautiful and immaculately kept. Much of the post we saw on the way in was composed of World War II buildings. We passed the modern Beach Army Hospital with a beautiful, HUEY Medevac helicopter sitting on the helipad poised to respond to any emergency. The Huey was a beautiful sight to behold.

We followed the directional signs to the 3rd WOC Company (WOC—Warrant Officer Candidate). The WOC companies were located in new three-story concrete block buildings. The messhall was a single story white concrete building that housed on the one side the messhall, and the other a little PX concession where upper classmen could get a beer, hamburger or pizza in the evening and the weekends.

A couple of other smaller one-story buildings were scattered about the area. These were briefing rooms where the candidates would meet their instructor daily for their pre-and post flight briefings. WOC hill overlooked the expansive heliport that at the time was the world's largest heliport. It would be a few long, hard weeks before we got to go to the heliport.

We reported in and were assigned three candidates to a room. Those candidates who had been sergeants and reported in with stripes and stuff were required to rip off their stripes immediately. Their rank was now Candidate, just like us 19 year olds who just graduated from basic training. We too were told we would have to exchange our standard enlisted "US" brass for the "W.O.C." brass.

From the very beginning everything was done at a double time. This meant you had to run everywhere being on your guard for senior candidates as everyone rated a salute. You had to answer everything with " Sir, Candidate Flanagan, yes sir!" Man this got old and we hadn't finished the first 1/2 of a day. We were issued our WOC Handbook, which specified how everything was to be in our rooms and on our uniforms. We were told to read it, learn it and follow it real quickly and explicitly.

Sometime during that first day or so we were given a shopping list and marched to the little PX Annex where we purchased our WOC Brass, orange felt backing to wear behind our brass and on our epaulets. We also purchased our unit baseball hats we wore in lieu of the army green hats we had worn in basic and the rest of the army wore. The color of the hats indicated the company you were assigned. And it indicated which phase of training you were in. This was very important because senior candidates rated a salute from the junior candidates. To not render the proper respect was cause for a verbal reprimand followed by a number of pushups. We were the Blue Hat class of Captain Merle Mulvaney's 3rd WOC Company.

Our class was going to be the biggest one they had ever formed at Fort Wolters. No doubt this was a reflection of the plan to significantly increase the US participation in the war in South Vietnam. We stretched into two buildings, not just the single building that the previous classes needed. After a couple days we were broken into platoons alphabetically. That put Rich Waldron in the other building. But for the first night we were hastily assigned to a platoon and a squad, and given initial room assignments.

Upon arriving in the rooms we began to empty our duffel bags and fold and roll all of our stuff according to the WOC Handbook. Underwear had to be rolled neatly and precisely so as to be six inches long and an inch in diameter, or some such other nonsense. Every so often a couple of senior candidates would come on the floor and fall (order) us out into the hallways. We would have to brace against the wall and wait while these guys ranted and raved. We would be given endless sets of pushups to do for some flagrant violation of the WOC Handbook. Often times the visits to the floor included an inspection of our progress in getting squared away. This resulted in all the stuff being unfolded because it didn't meet the exact requirement and the drawers were dumped over. This was endless. I recall sitting at the edge of my bunk shaking my head and asking myself, "What the f*ck have you gotten yourself into Flanagan." I seriously considered getting out of there immediately.

I don't know why I stayed that night. I could just leave and tell them I had made a mistake. Maybe I was just too tired and just wanted to sleep the night. I knew there would be plenty of time to quit the next day or the day after. Of course, maybe I stayed because I didn't want them to win?

I don't know why, but I stayed the course looking forward to the day before graduation so I could quit. That would show them who the smart one was. I wouldn't let them win.

Chapter Six

Best laid plans of mice and men. . . .

The routine of flight school caught on. The flying, pretty scary at first, became the big challenge. Priorities and attitudes change over very short periods of time when you look back on them.

The guys in the class were a great bunch. Man we had some real fun. If you want to read about the blow by blow adventures of a WOC's life read the book *Chicken Hawk* by Robert Mason. He tells the story of flight school better than I could. However I can't resist telling just a few stories about Blue Hat Class 66-23.

Each platoon had to develop its own identity and personality. Our platoon came up with a design for our helmets which had good ol'Snoopy astride a blue lightning bolt. Before we could use it, however, we had to get permission from the copyright holder. I think Al De Mailo and Bruce De Laurantis did the paperwork. In any case, in a short time we received permission to use it. We had the decals made up and we put them proudly on our shinny white helmets. I still have an extra decal of Snoopy. Before we could leave Fort Wolters however, our helmets had to be painted OD Green. They had found out the VC were using the white helmets as an aiming point. Reluctantly, we each had our buckets painted.

I clearly remember my first helicopter takeoff on my first

flight. I was flying the OH-23D Raven. A three-place observation helicopter manufactured by Hiller. The pilot sat in the center of the 3-seat bench with his legs straddling the instrument console. I remember when my instructor pilot (IP) sitting to my left first brought it to a hover. Wow, this was pretty neat. He hovered over to one of the eight or so takeoff pads and got clearance from the tower to takeoff. Because of the high density of helicopters large telephone poles painted different colors marked the takeoff and landing approach path to ensure separation from each other. As we took off, with no doors on the aircraft I could see the ground drop away as we began to climb. My stomach was a bit nervous with all of this. I am really afraid of heights. I first became aware of this when I would go up in the roof of the house to help my father tar the roof. I would go towards the edge of the roof and I would get that feeling in my stomach. On climb out I was getting that feeling again, and I didn't like it. After the first couple of hundred feet however I began to settle down and began listening to the IP as he was orienting me on the area around Fort Wolters.

We flew out to an area and the IP explained each of the controls one by one and what they did. He would demonstrate them first and then give me a chance to try it. First the cyclic, then the collective, followed by the pedals, and then the throttle. This was pretty easy, I thought to myself. Then he gave me all of the controls. This is not easy I said quickly. Everything was out of sorts in mere seconds. Helicopters are a constant balance of controls. If you change one control, just a little, you must make a change to the others. You must constantly be correcting the pitch, attitude, direction and power settings to keep the damn thing in the air. After enough of the humbling experience the IP took the controls again and let me settle down. This was repeated a number of times that first flight. I was doing okay with my fear of heights. Then my IP talked to me about autorotations. An autorotation is a flight maneuver used to safely land the aircraft after experiencing an in flight emergency, typically an engine failure.

In practicing autorotations at the stagefield the procedure is to line up on the autorotation lane (runway) at an altitude of five hundred feet. As the point of intended landing on the lane came into range you would cut the engine, reduce the collective pitch, apply almost full right pedal, and maintain a certain prescribed airspeed. Once established in the descent you would check to ensure that the main rotor speed was in the green operating range, and the airspeed was as desired. Passing through 100 feet you would decelerate the helicopter by raising its nose. This accomplished two things; first, it increased the speed of the rotor blades and second, it slowed its forward movement. This attitude was held until about ten feet when you would pull pitch. That is change the pitch of the blades thereby checking the rate of descent and decreasing the forward speed dramatically. As the speed and descent dissipated you would level the aircraft (in the OH23 you did this, in the TH55 and Huey you remained in the decelerating attitude) and gently cushion the landing by applying more pitch. Once you touched down you maintained heading with the pedals and the cyclic, until finally you came to a halt. All this would happen in mere seconds.

After explaining the concept, he demonstrated an autorotation. I can not tell you how I felt when he cut that engine and we began to drop. Like the drop on the first hill of the Cyclone roller coaster in Coney Island, I wanted to scream and hold on. I was not a fan of roller coasters at all, and this was very much like a roller coaster. We climbed back to altitude and he did it again. Climbing back to altitude he cleared the area below us, gave me the controls, and said it's your turn now. I still didn't like the feeling in my stomach, but I felt better when I was in control.

It took some time but I gradually got over the fear of heights in a helicopter. I still don't like high places like roofs and tall ladders, but I am fine in aircraft.

Cleared Solo Of all the things in primary flight school that sticks in my memory the most are the days that I first soloed a helicopter and the day I soloed in autorotations.

We knew when the day for soloing was drawing near. Our flight hours were building. As you approached the 10 or 12 hour level you should be ready to solo. First one or two would solo in a day, and then the numbers grew, and decreased again as the last in the class were set loose. I certainly was not the first to solo, nor the last. I was in the middle.

I had had a couple of tough flight periods with my IP before this one particular day. Finally, after flying about an hour and twenty minutes of the scheduled two hour flight period, he told me to hover taxi over to the side and he got out. As he was securing his seat belt so it wouldn't blow around or foul the controls, he reminded me of all the things I needed to do. Then he wished me good luck and sent me solo. I don't know if I really wanted him to leave me.

I cannot describe the feeling or the thrill of picking that OH-23D up to a hover and taxing out for take-off. After picking it to the hover, everything else was a piece of cake. I did my three take-offs and landings, then taxied to the ramp and shut it down. My IP met me in the stagefield house and debriefed me. From there on flying was much easier for me.

Before we graduated from the second phase of primary training we also had to demonstrate our proficiency by soloing in autorotations. In a helicopter the angle of the glide is very steep compared to a fixed wing airplane where the glide ratio is pretty good. In a helicopter when you lose the engine you look for a landing spot right in front or under you.

When my IP got out and cleared me to solo for autorotation, I didn't know whether he was doing me any favor or not. It seemed an unnatural thing for me to cut the throttle on myself.

I went around the first time and after a bit of hesitation I finally cut the throttle. As soon as I heard the engine RPMs go down I did as I was taught and talked my way through the procedure to touchdown. The touchdown was really smooth. Even my instructor commented over the radio saying how nice a job I had done. Big headed, I showboated to and through the takeoff and traffic pattern. I came to the proper point and cut the throttle and came down like a champ. I flared at a 100', pulled initial pitch at 10', leveled the aircraft and pulled pitch again. Ops! This popped me back up in the air again. Oh shit! I reduced the pitch and flared again, as the helicopter came through five feet, I gently nursed the remaining pitch. (The blades had only so much inertia in them. As you loaded the blades the inertia was reduced. If you pulled too much the blades would slow to a point of ineffectiveness.) I got it down on the ground and skidded for a long ways. Heart pounding, I took inventory. Nothing damaged, but my ego.

I meekly called for clearance to taxi and takeoff. Humbled, I then flew the most professional traffic pattern I could, and made a better autorotation than the first. When I met my IP after shutdown, he asked me if I learned anything on the second autorotation. I told him I had learned big heads don't fly too well. I learned that lesson again a few years later. But that's another series of tales.

Long Weekend Weekend passes depended on the candidate performing his tasks to certain level of proficiency. Levels of proficiency were tracked in the form of "merits" and "demerits." The fewer demerits through the week the longer your pass privileges were on the weekend. The longer you were in school the fewer demerits were allowed. After the first few weeks of preflight I realized that I probably would never get a weekend off. I had tried a couple of times, but it always seemed that the Friday inspection would just put me over the limit and I would find myself pushing a lawn mower or some such character building detail for the first sergeant.

Something happened and I found myself with a pass for a long weekend. I had kept in touch with Tom Jennings and knew he was at Laughlin AFB, in Del Rio, Texas. Laughlin was a pilot training base for the Air Force. Tom was a jet engine mechanic there. I called Tom and he said he was available for the weekend and that they had BEQs (Bachelor Enlisted Quarters) available for us. Russ Doersam an older cadet, was a farmer from Upper Sandusky Ohio, and he had a car. He would drive. Rich Waldron came along as well. The drive from Mineral Wells Texas, located just west of Fort Worth, to Del Rio which bordered Mexico, was a long one. Though the excitement of being away from the base for a few days and seeing Tommy again made the drive bearable.

We got there and were stopped at the gate by the Air Force Security Police. We presented our IDs and told the guard we were army flight students stationed at Fort Wolters. The guy gave us a temporary visitor's sticker for the car, saluted us, and directed us to the BOQ. This was the bachelors officer's quarters. There, we were told that flight candidates were treated as officers in the Air Force. Boy, I'm gonna like it here. They salute us! We were very much tempted to do a U-turn and enter again just to get another salute. We didn't though.

We caught up to Tom and went to his room. Their barracks were similar to the ones we had at Wolters. Relatively new, three story buildings with dayrooms on each floor. The rooms were the same size, except that Tom only had one roommate, whereas we had three candidates to a room. Obviously the Air Force didn't share the Army's standards for cleanliness and order of the barracks. Tom's room was an absolute mess by Army standards. I really envied Tom his room was a lot more comfortable and livable than our highly polished and sterile rooms back at Wolters.

Tom headed us up and we drove across the border to go to the bullfights. The Base had established a "Juan Valdez Club." You paid five dollars to join. This entitled you to sit in the fan club section of the arena. The club did everything opposite to the normal customs of traditional bullfighting. First the fan club was in the sunny section of the arena a definite no-no to the aficionados of the sport. Next we were to applaud neither the matador nor the bull. In fact we were to wait until after the bull had been killed and drug out of the stadium. That was to be the signal to get ready. For as the bull was being readied for the exit, Juan Valdez, dressed in a white matadors costume, festooned with gold embroidery, with his named blazoned on the back of his shirt would enter the arena. The fan club would rise from its bleachers and begin to cheer wildly as Juan pushed his wheelbarrow about the arena cleaning up the excrement, blood and flesh the bull might have deposited in the ring. As Juan exited the ring the club would cheer again and Juan would tip his hat and bow to his admiring fans. Did I mention that a part of the dues included all the margaritas you could drink from the large messhall water coolers the club furnished?

We continued partying across the border well into the night. We lost Russ for a while and began a search of the local area. I found him sitting at a small table in a small local bar with two Mexican men drinking tequila. They were having a great time, despite Russ not knowing a word of Spanish and they not speaking much understandable English. We left there and only God knows how we made it back alive.

We went to Mexico the next night too. This time we went to a place referred to as Boy's Town. Father Flanagan would change the name of his place if he knew what went on here in this other place called "Boy's Town." I finally found the origins of the term "a dog and pony show." While there we were offered the chance to meet a number of Mexican sisters. We got out of there alive too. Somebody was certainly watching over us.

The trip home seemed longer. I am sure the hangovers and lack of sleep and good food for the last few days had a lot to do with it. We arrived back at the orderly room with barley moments to spare before we would be officially late. I had a bit of problem that needed to be solved before I got ready for the next day.

After one of the bullfights I went under the stands where they slaughter the bull and sell or give the meat away. I bought one set of the bull's horns for twenty bucks. Now I needed someplace to keep them until I could clean the remaining skull and brains off of them. Since we got back from pass so late I didn't have time to find a place, so I put them in my security locker, which is a an area above the built in wall lockers which can be locked separately. A few days later I put the horns out back of one of the briefing rooms across from the mess hall. I figured that in a couple of days the ants and night animals would have cleaned them up pretty well. I went back in three days but the horns were gone. I don't know what happened to them. Oh well, I don't know what I would have done with them all these years anyway,

Mail Call One day I received a strange letter in my mailbox. The return address indicated it came from a girl who lived across the street from my cousins in Howard Beach, New York. The girl said she decided to write to one of Gerry's (my cousin) cousins in the service. This girl, who signed her letters "Snooks," chose to write to me. I replied to the letter with a proposal of marriage. Though Snooks doesn't remember this part of my initial letter back to her. This began a long distance relationship through the mail. I would get a letter or a card almost every day from Snooks. She sent me a picture after a few weeks of writing. The picture showed me a cute girl with dark glasses and fashionably cut short blonde hair.

At the time though I was also corresponding with a couple of other girls I had known or dated before I was drafted. I thank them all and each of them for their thoughtfulness. Terry, a former candy stripper and long time friend kept me up to date on every Batman show. I'll bet she ended up summarizing almost every script ever written for the series. Or so it would seem. I very much enjoyed reading about Batman but enjoyed reading Snooks' letters and cards more. This Snooks person was different. We started to write to each other most every day. She was really easy to converse with, and seemed to be a really neat, honest person. So much so, that when we had graduated from the primary helicopter school and were being held over for a month at Fort Wolters,

I took an extended weekend pass and went back to NY. My return home was going to be a surprise for everyone. I didn't tell anyone back home that I was coming in.

I got home and knocked at the door to my house. Stupid me I had forgotten to bring the key. I could see my Mom glancing through the curtains in the living room as she almost ran to the door. My Mom came to the door, and was shaking as she opened the door. I thought she had seen a ghost. She was almost crying and was shaking all over. I asked her "what was wrong?" She told me that all she could see was the uniform and she immediately thought I had been killed and this was the official notification party. I felt so dumb. I never, ever thought about me being killed. I made a promise right then that I would never wear a uniform to my Mom's house without first telling her I was coming home.

On Saturday afternoon I called Snooks and made arrangements for us and my cousin and my buddy Denis to go out that night. (Denis was the last guy of our group. Denis didn't go into the service like the rest of us. He went to St. John's University Medical School. He's a doctor practicing medicine in Los Angeles today.) I needed Denis to drive the car. I had just gotten my first license in Texas, but didn't have any insurance coverage. Denis did. Snooks really wasn't up to going out, but she said yes anyway. The problem was she had had two wisdom teeth pulled that morning. We met and went out and struck it off pretty well. We went to Coney Island and had some of those great Nathan's Frankfurters and French-fries.

Details I got back to Fort Wolters, late, but no one seemed to notice. I couldn't get there and back within the 72-hour time limit of the pass. The Fish, Al De Mailo, answered "Here" for me at the formations, so no one really knew I wasn't there. Not being found out was a good thing because technically I was absent without official leave—AWOL. I could have been kicked out of flight school had I been found out. More probably I would have been fined and restricted to the post for a month or two. Regardless of the punishment it would been a permanent mark on my record. We were held over at Fort Wolters for about a month until Fort Rucker could accept us. The war was reaching its height and our class was just too big for Fort Rucker to accommodate us all at once. In any case we were held over for a month and they needed to find work for us to do. During that time we pulled all kinds of work details. On one of the details we were sent out on parade fields shoulder to shoulder and told to pick up rocks that were larger than 2 inches in diameter. When after a couple of full days we finished that, we were sent back out and to pick up rocks larger than 1.5 inches in diameter. Got the picture? By the time we had finished that series of details there were no rocks of any size on the parade field.

Another detail was much more sobering. With the increases in Vietnam came increased casualties. We had to be ready to send out up to four or five burial details a day. I went on a number of these details. Luckily I always drew the firing squad (as a member of the firing team, not a target). We just stayed in the vans most of the time except when the body was being moved from place to place, and then when we fired the salute at the graveside. The poor guys who were the pallbearers spent most of their time inside. One time I was especially glad to be on the outside.

This was a funeral for a black soldier. Since there were only two black guys in our class, the majority of the details were white only, as was this one. The soldier was laid out in a downtown funeral home and then was moved to a rural, really rural black church. The small, weather worn, simple country church was a long ways down a dirt road. Cars were parked all over the shoulders of the road. There was a heavy smell of liquor as the family and the other parishioners passed us. We went to the vans, but the pallbearers were inside in the front pews.

I don't have any idea what was happening inside, all we could hear was loud music and singing and voices shouting and screaming. Occasionally we would hear a woman wailing loudly. Man I was glad I wasn't in there. And the service went on forever. Finally we got the high sign that the service was about to end. He was being buried in the little graveyard adjacent to the church. We went back there. The graveyard was not orderly laid out as the cemeteries I had always seen. This place had graves at every angle imaginable, and tombstones of every kind. A fence made of multi-strand wire boarded the graveyard. We arranged ourselves as the burial detail ready for the casket and the family.

Our guys brought the casket out and were carrying it through the graveyard to the gravesite followed by the family and the parishioners. The grave was pretty close to the fence and a big crooked tree with surface roots above the ragged grass turf, necessitating a 90-degree turn with not much room. As our lead pallbearer on the left side was making the turn he slipped and his right leg almost went in the grave with the casket on top of him. Luckily, he was able to maintain his balance and didn't drop the casket.

We got through the service and gave him a good professional and sincere send off, and I think the family was satisfied with our performance.

As we talked in the van on the way back from that funeral, the guys who were inside said that the ceremony was really scary. There were people falling on the floor, and screaming and talking loudly. I made up my mind to never be a pallbearer if I could help it. I also made up my mind to tell my family that at my burial to make sure they threw a case of beer in the burial team's van and tell them I wanted them to have it.

Rucker and Bust The holdover month did finally come to an end and we were allowed to leave for Fort Rucker Alabama. Rich and I had decided to stop off in New Orleans and visit the French Quarter. We went in his little red Volkswagen bug. We got to New Orleans, checked into a hotel and drove to the Quarter, parking the car on a street a couple of blocks off the main drag. We had a great time walking up the street, visiting Patty O'Briens, and lots of other places. We had had quite a few drinks, but that was over an extended period of time so we weren't drunk or anything near that way.

We got back to the car finally about 2:30 in the morning. As we approached the car something didn't look right. When we got alongside of it we realized someone had broken into the car and taken everything out of the car. Everything that is, except for our flight helmets. What a way to go! We reported the incident it the police, but they were not very optimistic that our stuff would be recovered.

This would make reporting in to Fort Rucker a bit difficult, since we needed to be in uniform and the ones we had left in the motel were gross. Living in one set of clothes for about three days made them even more gross. Man did I smell badly. We finally got the reports done and got a new issue from the clothing sales store on credit. We were told the charges for the new issue would be taken out of our pay. The NCOs (non-commissioned officers, or sergeants) in charge of the issue point were sympathetic about what happened and helped us out a lot. The charges never did show up on my pay voucher. I thank those supply sergeants who-ever they were for losing that paperwork. It still cost a lot of money buying patches and nametags and having them sewn on. But the sewing charge was a lot cheaper than paying for an entire new issue of clothes. Starting out at a new base after being robbed of everything you had was a real bummer.

Chapter Seven

Fort Rucker—The Home of Army Aviation

Fort Rucker Alabama was, and still is, the home of Army Aviation. Here in 1966 the sky filled with helicopters and airplanes everyday of the week and all day and night long. For us candidates things got a bit easier at Rucker. They treated us less like trainees and dummies and more like adults.

Our training changed also. We now entered the instrument phase of training where we learned how to fly under instrument flight rules. To do this they attached a set of blinders to our helmets that they called a hood and which blocked our vision of the outside world. All we could see were the instruments. The instruments told us about what the aircraft was doing. How fast we were going up or down. How high we were. What our airspeed was. Whether we were in trim. How fast and what direction we were turning. And what the relationship was of our nose and "wings" to the horizon.

There was much to learn in addition to the flight skills. There were instruments with needles and pointers on them that gave us information on where the radio navigation stations were in relation to where we were, or what we set the dials to tell us.

The vertical speed indicator, the altimeter, airspeed indicator, turn and slip indicators and horizontal indicator told us about the aircraft, and the navigation radios and instruments told us where our aircraft was in relation to the invisible highways in the sky.

There were all kinds of rules to learn. There were rules on who to talk to on the radio and when, and what to say, in what order, and it changed depending on whether you were in radar contact or not in radar contact.

I was having a lot of trouble with the basic instrument phase of the training. I don't know what the reason for this was I just had trouble getting it all done at the right time. I was one of the last ones to go for my end of phase check-ride. These check-rides were given by a separate group of instructor pilots, whose sole purpose was to evaluate student pilots. And I guess indirectly the regular teaching IPs. In any case I was put up for my check ride. That morning my IP got the list, which listed who my check-pilot was to be. My IP was upset. He told me the check pilot I had drawn was the toughest guy of them all, and that I should not worry, that I would probably "bust" the ride, but that he would put me back up two days later. He went on to say that the good thing about busting a ride with this guy, would mean I would never have to fly with him again.

I went down to the check ride room and met the check pilot. We went out and flew the check ride. It went pretty well to my mind. I didn't come close to killing us, and I found him rather helpful. The check ride was a lot less stressful than a normal flight period with my regular instructor, and the time seemed to go by pretty quick. When we got on the ground the check-pilot gave me a quick debrief and I went back to my regular IP.

When I got there my IP told me he had me scheduled for my second ride the day after next. I told him that I had thought I heard the Check Pilot say I passed. My IP looked at me in disbelief and asked me what grade did he say? I told him I thought he said something about a 96. My IP couldn't or didn't believe me and left the room to go see the check pilot. He returned in about ten minutes and told me he didn't know how I did it but I did get a 96 on the ride.

We all took basic instruments in the Bell TH-13T. This is the bubble type helicopter that you would usually see on M.A.S.H. Ours was a later model and had been specially converted to meet the instrument training program. In advanced instruments a portion of the class used A and B model Hueys. My group however, used TH13Ts the whole time.

Our instrument training was broken by the Christmas holidays in December 1966. The post closed down from around the 20th of December to the 3rd of January.

Christmas 1966 Snooks and I had more to write about to each other between the weekend I went home from Wolters and Christmas. When the holiday vacation came, I made plans to see her more often. Since I now had my license, Hannah and Bill lent me their Chevy II Nova Station wagon so I could take Snooks out. The first night we went out we came back by my house so that I could introduce Snooks to my Mom and father. It was late, so I went in the house and left her in the car. I went in and found they already gone to bed. I went back to the car and told Snooks we would do it the next night. I dropped Snooks off at her house in Howard Beach and came back to my house in Brooklyn.

The next morning my Mom, excitedly, woke me up looking scared and saying that she couldn't wake my father up. I went in and found he was not breathing, I told Mom to call the police and an ambulance. I attempted mouth to mouth for a bit, but he was already cold and lifeless. The police arrived and with just a quick look and touch said "he's dead." I told my Mom and she began to cry. I led her down the stairs and told her to wait there. I went back upstairs and told my Grandmother and brought her downstairs to wait with my Mother. My Uncle Dave came over and stayed with them. I called Hannah and told her I would be over early and needed her to come back to Brooklyn with me. I drove to Staten Island to bring the car over so she could bring us back to Brooklyn. I didn't tell her he was dead until I got to her house, and then we came back to Brooklyn.

Snooks and my plans for the vacation were changed now. The centerpiece for the holidays was now a wake and a funeral. I was with Mom when we picked out the coffin and made the funeral arrangements. This was not how I planned to spend my Christmas. My father screwed this up for me too.

I saw a lot of people at the funeral; including each of the girls who I had been corresponding with. In fact, they all came the same afternoon, as well as a couple of girls I had gone to school with. I almost made it through okay without them running into each other, until Terry had trouble getting her winter boots on, and Snooks showed up a few minutes early. I introduced them to each other, and hustled Terry out of the funeral home. I am thankful that the girls took the time to come to the funeral home for my family, and me but it could have turned out much differently had they all showed up at the same time.

Everything wasn't perfect with Snooks when she came in. You see my sister Hannah and family picked Snooks up and drove her in to the funeral home. When she got in the car Hannah introduced Snooks to her daughters. Terry my niece and god-daughter looked at Snooks and said "You're not Uncle John's girlfriend, Linda is." Hannah almost killed Terry for saying that. Snooks told me about it in no uncertain terms and told me she didn't like Terry at all. Her feelings have changed a lot since that first encounter. You can't blame the girls though. Linda and I dated for so long and we spent a lot of time with Hannah and Bill, she was part of the family.

Snooks and I did get some time to talk and see each other. We got time to be together and to be alone with each other. We got very serious very quickly. But you know we had written to each other most every day and we really knew a lot about each other. We did decide right before I left to go back to Fort Rucker that we would get engaged when I graduated in March, and then get married in April the following year when I got home from

Vietnam. I asked her father and he said "All right, take good care of my baby." We then told my family. They were surprised and thought that we were rushing into things. They thought that we should wait until I got back from Vietnam to set a date. We didn't take their advice we knew what we wanted to do.

1967 Back to Rucker I had no real problem after getting back to Rucker. Training picked up some and began to become more interesting. Although we had undergone 50 hours of instrument training, the Army would not give us standard instrument tickets which would allow us to intentionally fly in instrument conditions outside of the tactical (read combat) area. We were issued "pink" tickets or tactical instrument tickets, good only in Vietnam.

After the instrument phase we entered the tactical phase of training and became senior candidates. As senior candidates we traded one set of collar brass for the U.S. brass of an Officer to denote that our next step would be to become an officer in the United States Army. It may not sound like much now, but it meant a lot to me back then.

During the tactical phase of training we would be transitioned into each model of the Huey—A, B, B model with the 540-rotor system, C and D model. In this phase we got to finally fly the Cadillac of helicopters—the Huey. The Huey was a fine aircraft. I would begin a life long love affair with this bird. Even today when I hear the telltale sounds of the Huey's blades I stop and look up at her with love. We would also be checked out on the various gun systems and allowed to make a few passes on the aerial gun range. This was fun. Flying low level at high speed, down the winding river in lower Alabama and blasting away with four machine guns at the targets. Seeing the tracers running out ahead of the aircraft and impacting in the dirt and the water and finally hitting the target. The sound of the guns, the smell of the firing, the excitement, wow! This is good.

They did not let us fire the rockets though. I would have to wait for that until I got in country. The tactical phase of training was capped off by a one week in the field exercise at TAC X. TAC X was a field site made to look and run as a base camp in Vietnam. There we flew simulated tactical missions. Most of these missions were performed without an instructor, just two candidates. The missions were realistic, and flown low level. And the living in the field was fun too.

After the Tactical week we had a week of final check rides. Each day a certain number of candidates would take their final check ride, and if they passed it would be the last time they would fly as a student pilot. It also signaled the end of training, which meant that you didn't have to get up and go to the flight line. Al De Mailo, Dave Foster, Bob Edwards and I all completed our check rides on the same day and went to the club to celebrate. Boy, did we have a great time. Coming back from the club we decided we would pull our last prank on our platoon mates.

The barracks we stayed in were old World War II barracks which had been modified to provide two room suites. Each suite had two rooms. One room was for sleeping, the other for our desks and lockers. The doors had hasps on the outside, so you could padlock the doors closed for security when you left the area. Some of these hasps had been removed or kicked in when one or the other roommate was unable to open the lock.

We decided to wire the hasps and lock the doors from the outside of our platoon mates to make it difficult for them to get out the next morning. To cast suspicion wider than ourselves, we also chose to not wire a random number of doors. Thus the likely culprits numbered more than just the four of us. We laughed quietly and snickered while we set about wiring the doors closed. We then hit the rack. I laughed myself to sleep. Albeit a short sleep however.

Early the next morning, guys yelling and banging on doors awakened us. People were yelling and cursing and really upset. The guys who would take their check rides that day were particularly concerned. Those who were not wired in came to the rescue and released the hangers from the hasps. The platoon went wild with many swearing oaths to kill those bastards who were responsible. We were certain it had to be somebody from another class who decided to play this prank. The secret stayed among Bob, Dave, The Fish and me for a very long time.

In retrospect we did a really foolish and dangerous stunt. If there had been a fire we could have been responsible for someone's death. We were lucky, and no one was hurt, and no one busted his final check ride either. But this was a dumb thing to do. Funny at the time, but dumb!

At Long Last—Graduation On 13 March 1967, at Fort Rucker Alabama, WORWAC Class 67-1 graduated from Flight School. Each member of the class was sworn in as Warrant Officer 1s. There was a short break or intermission in the ceremony and then we were awarded the wings signifying we were now Army Aviators.

US Army Aviator Wings

Tradition or rumor held that you shouldn't wear the wings you were first awarded for it would bring bad luck. These "blood wings" should be exchanged among awardees so that you would never wear them by accident. Dave Foster and I exchanged wings immediately after the ceremony. Another tradition was the dollar salute. Custom said that the first person to render you a salute after being commissioned or upon receiving a warrant the new officer was to give the person a dollar. Let me tell you that after graduation there were a number of sergeants who were determined to get rich by saluting the new "misters." I ducked these guys, opting to pin my WOC brass through a dollar bill and return to the WOC area and give it to the first WOC who gave me a salute. It didn't take long.

I went to check my mailbox for the last time at Rucker and on the way in ran into two CW2s (Chief Warrant Officers). Seeing them I snapped a smart candidate salute on them and sounded off "Good Afternoon Sir!" They looked at me and then looked at each other and shook their heads. I then realized I was a warrant officer, and warrant officers didn't salute each other. I was to learn later that warrant officers don't like to salute many people.

In 1967 when I graduated from flight school there were four grades of Warrant Officer. Warrant Officer One was the junior rack and the officer was addressed as Mister. The ranks above the junior grade were addressed as Chief Warrant Officer 2, 3, or 4, as appropriate. Some of the older warrants took offense to folks, especially RLOs (Real Live Officers as commissioned officers were often referred to as), calling them "Chief." The comeback would often be "Chief? I am not an Indian; I'm a Warrant Officer."

I was happy being called a Mister, it sounded much better than "private," "candidate" or anything else I had been called over my short, but intense, army career.

My Mom and Aunt Florence (one of my father's sisters) came down and witnessed the graduation ceremony, and attended the graduation formal the night before.

I don't know exactly when I changed my mind and decided not to quit the day before graduation. I guess after working so hard to stay in school and learn to fly, and really getting to the point where I enjoyed the idea of flying being an Army helicopter pilot, it just seemed the right thing to do. And besides I had made it where so many others had yearned to be and didn't make it, or died trying to get here. I was finally something—a helicopter pilot. I liked the thought of that. Despite what the nuns used to tell me about not making anything of myself; and all the self doubting and insecurity I had growing up, I was now something.

A helicopter pilot. And that was something great. But I knew I was also still John, with all that comes with.

When we got home my bags had missed the plane in Atlanta, so I had to wait a few extra hours before I could give Snooks her engagement ring. Mom was really nervous that I would never see my bags again. After all the training I had been through in the last year, and knowing what and where I was about to go in a few weeks, a lost bag was a "non-problem."

I do hope it's really the thought that counts, the diamond isn't very big in the engagement ring. Someday I'll win the lottery and buy her a big one if she wants it. It has lasted 33 years so far, thanks to her being such a good person and not giving up on me. And for her not giving up on us.

Chapter Eight

Good-bye USA

When we graduated from Fort Rucker we were told we would be contacted at our leave address and be given a "port call." A port call is an order or instruction telling us when to report to a place where our overseas journey will officially begin and we will leave the country. As soon as I got mine I made my flight arrangements for San Francisco. From there we would have to take a bus to Travis Air Force Base.

Arriving at the San Francisco airport I ran into several of my classmates and we decided to wait in the bar until time to catch the bus for Travis. As we waited, other classmates showed up and joined us. While we waited I was taken at the situation. Here we were sitting in a bar in our home country waiting to leave to fight our country's war, as officers flying helicopters with 13 souls on board and our country thought we were too young to either buy a drink in California or vote in any election. No one questioned our ages at the bar, and I thank them for it. I wonder what would have happened if we had been arrested for underage drinking on that day in San Francisco? Would they not let us go to Vietnam? Or maybe they wouldn't let us back? Who knew? Who really cared?

The bus ride was a bit longer than I had thought it would be. But no problem, as we sat in the back of the bus I poured drinks for my buddies from my portable bar. Thankfully the bus did have an on-board rest room which we frequented often.

We didn't get to leave for Vietnam as scheduled. The aircraft we were supposed to fly overseas on had some mechanical failure and we were put up in some budget motel for the night. This didn't seem to be the right way to open a new chapter in life. One of the problems we had though was that we had already checked our bags with the military so we didn't have anything to change into.

The next day we took off in our day old uniforms, in the crowded, maximum seating capacity stretched DC9s that the contract carrier was using to haul GIs to Vietnam. Our flight was going to take us up to Alaska for refueling then on to Japan (Yokota) and the Philippines, and finally into Bien Hoa. We would have to de-plane on each of these stops so they could refuel the plane safely. We checked at the gate in Alaska if there was a bar and how far was it. As it turned out the bar was way on the other side of the facility. We ran through a maze of cold, temporary walkways until we reached the bar. We had a few beers before we walked back to the plane.

We refueled in Yakota Japan. We were taken off the airplane in the cold darkness of the night and put in a hanger while the aircraft was refueling. Standing at the door of the hanger my thoughts raced and my eyes looked deep into space for answers or assurances, or something. Was I good enough? Would I be able to do what I needed to do? What is it going to be like? How am I going to feel? How is this going to turn out? Why? No help there, no answers, no assurances. Though there were probably 200 guys in the hanger around me, I was lonely. Is this how it is going to be? No time for answers now the refueling was over; we get on the plane and continued heading west.

Next stop "The Republic of South Vietnam" As the aircraft made its approach into the airport I thought of a thousand things. The not knowing of what was going to happen, what was I going to do, what I could control, and what lay ahead, gave me an unreal feeling that gripped my whole insides. The approach into Bien Hoa was steep for a commercial airliner shooting a traffic pattern, I thought. Then I realized, of course its steep, the bad guys may be around there and might want to take a pot shot at us. Welcome to Vietnam and a new reality.

We filed off the airplane, tired and groggy from the long flight and also reacting to the extreme heat assaulting our bodies. We were greeted with cheers and jeers from the crowd of soldiers waiting to board our aircraft for their return flight to the land of the "Big PX." What a contrast! Here they were excitedly waiting to board the plane to go home with full anticipation of reuniting with loved ones left behind a life time ago, while we were entering a period of severe unknown. Neither knew of the future, but shortly both would share a past.

I could hardly believe that we were in fact on the other side of the world. And we were scheduled to stay here for the next twelve months. Twelve months earlier I was in the third week of basic training, and now I was a pilot, and in Vietnam. That was a long time ago as I looked back on basic training and all that had happened in between, and now I had the same time laying ahead of me in this hot, dry, dangerous, and lonely place half way around the world.

"What the hell are you doing here Flanagan?" I kept asking myself.

Light antitank Weapon LAW—CAV School As I mentioned before the Colonel who had "blessed us" answered many of the questions I had on my arrival to the Republic of Vietnam (RVN). Now the question was how long do I have to wait for the inevitable? I made up my mind to not worry about the small shit; and resigning yourself to dying in Vietnam put most things in the small stuff category. I decided I didn't want to go any sooner than I had to, and wanted to help as many folks get back as I could.

Before going forward to join our units, the 1st CAV presented an indoctrination course at An Khe for everyone assigned to the division. The school was mainly for the grunts and the enlisted men. We found this out and spent most of the three-day school on more important things, like exploring the neighboring village of An Khe.

We did learn something during this time at An Khe. We got to meet first hand that gung ho lieutenant from the C130 who was so afraid someone would have to wait and take the next flight. He was Lieutenant Ted Chilcote, our new infantry platoon leader—the new "Blue." I didn't know if I was gonna like being around this guy. Though as it turned out, Blue was super—a great leader who took care of his troops. The troops loved him and respected him totally. He stayed in the army and retired as a full colonel.

We did take one briefing I remember. We were sitting in the bleachers listening to a sergeant droning on about this thing that looked like an oversized paper towel cylinder. They called it a LAW, a light anti-tank weapon. The LAW is fired from the shoulder and propelled by a rocket motor. It looked like a compact, collapsible and lighter version of the old bazooka. He mentioned good old Newton's law—for every action there is an opposite and equal reaction. Here he was speaking of the dynamics of the rocket. When launched the rocket's motor would ignite and propel the missile at some incredible speed towards the target. He applied Newton's law and told us about the danger zone caused by the equal speed of the back blast behind the weapon when the rocket motor ignites. The back blast radius is a pretty big area. The time came and our attention was directed to a soldier off to our right front with a LAW on his shoulder. Then we were directed to look at the target, a truck I think, down range and to our left front. He gave a couple of more words and then said over the PA system fire when ready.

The firing soldier began to extend the rocket tube and place it on his shoulder—I saw it! I noticed it! There was a sergeant walking towards us on a direct line from the other side of the danger zone. Surely this was a set-up I thought. Teach me to think. Just then I heard the sound of the LAW firing and saw the sergeant fold to the ground. He had been hit by the back blast. The sergeant giving the class realized what had happened and quickly reset his radio. We could hear him call for a Medevac. The Medevac was there in what seemed to be seconds, and the injured sergeant was air lifted out. To this day I don't know for sure, whether that was really an accident or a set up to drive home the need for caution.

As I think back I also recall seeing my first demo of FUGAS that day. FUGAS was a combination of fuels, explosives, and metal stuff that was buried about the perimeter. If the red horde decided to come through the wire the command detonated FUGAS would blow the hell out of them.

This was going to be some experience I told myself.

Sin City, An Khe The An Khe "Sin City" orientation also proved very beneficial. Sin City was a closed square compound with shops around the inside perimeter of the walls and another set of shops that faced these from the center of the square. Most of the shops were bars and steam baths; but I think there were a few souvenir shops as well. The only entrance to Sin City was through a gate that was manned by MPs. No vehicles were allowed in the compound except the medics and the folks who delivered the beer. The MPs made sure only US troops and personnel who had been cleared to work there were allowed past the checkpoint. If I am not mistaken enlisted and NCOs had to leave their weapons at the checkpoint and retrieve them on the way out. I think officers and warrant officers were allowed to keep their pistols with them.

The main purpose of the City was to give the GI a safe place to let off some steam and to keep the Division's VD rate down. Each bar had a different theme or catered to a different segment of the Cav Troopers. As you strolled down the dirt street, you could hear the different kinds of music blasting out through the doorways of the bars. Inside the bars an endless group of young bar girls waited to entertain the troops in exchange for buying them Saigon tea. Saigon tea was either cold tea or diluted Coca-Cola that was priced very high compared to the beer the GI's mostly drank. But the cost of having the young girls play around was well worth it, or so it seemed. For those who wanted more there was a mama-san there to work the deal.

I understand that the CAV's medic checked the bargirls in Sin City at least weekly and that the 1st Cav had one of the lowest VD rates. That is until a report on Sin City was done by 60 Minutes after I left. The CAV was accused of running a city of ill repute and the mothers of the nation rose up and objected to it. I visited the city on my second tour after the Cav had moved on and the Fourth Division took over An Khe. The MPs on the checkpoint were gone and the place looked like a slum.

In any case, Sin City was the first time I had ever had a steam bath and massage. We would bring in a pail of cold water at the start and set it on the floor. When the steam got so hot you couldn't take it anymore you would pour the water over your head so you could last a little longer. The massages were wonderful. These little Vietnamese women would pound forever on your back and extremities and then even climb on top of the table and walk up and down your back massaging it with their expert feet and toes. The feeling was truly wonderful!

We also learned to never pay the price that was quoted, or marked on an item. Everything—believe me, everything—was negotiable.

I enjoyed the rides in the village. They had these little 3 wheeled Lambrettas that had a passenger compartment in the back that had bench seats facing each other. They were designed for 8 or so Vietnamese. We could squeeze in about four comfortably or six barely. Many of time we drag raced other Lambrettas promising our driver a bonus if we got to the gate or other destination ahead of the others.

An Khe had a little bit of everything. They had all sorts of laundries and embroidery shops and places where you could pick up souvenirs. There were also those massage parlors and steam baths that specialized in very personal relaxation services. Or so I am told.

I always had fun going into An Khe. Going into the city was always an adventure, you were never quite sure what you would see. I cannot recall anyone ever getting shot or hurt in the city.

In-country Checkout After "completing" the CAV's FNG (F*cking New Guy) school we were flown by Huey up to LZ Two Bits; actually Two Bits North. Two Bits was about a forty-minute flight as I recall. The LZ was situated on the Bong Son plain that met the South China Sea on the east. Bong Son was the northern most area of II Corps. The flight took you north from An Khe up the mountains and through a narrow saddle pass at the top, where the highway to Qui Nhon and places north and east ran. You had to be careful coming though the narrow pass at the top of the saddle during periods of bad weather and low ceilings, because everybody flew over the road and through the pass. Jim Pratt and I almost met an Air Force Caribou (C7A) head on one day. Luckily we both obeyed the rules of the road and stayed on the right side of the highway!

After clearing the An Khe pass you entered into some valleys that bore the scars of hard Cav fighting. There were no villages left, the area still showed the signs of napalm and heavy bomb and artillery damage, and there were some partially destroyed pagodas, as well as an abandoned fire base or two. The valleys gave way to the expanse of the Bong Son plain, with the South China Sea to the east, and the mouth of the An Lo Valley to the west. Just north of the river that ran down the An Lo and emptied in the sea, Two Bits was situated.

The LZ had two distinct, but adjacent sections, north and south. The north section, was where the 1/9th Squadron Headquarters had set up its forward base. Two of our sister troops were still collocated with the headquarters. B Troop had just recently moved north to Duc Pho. The area was covered with helicopter revetments. Scattered between the revetments were areas where you could land and take off. These areas were neither runways, nor take off pads. They were just long areas where you could form up and take off in somewhat of a normal manner. In one area of the LZ tents were arranged in rows. Each tent had sandbags piled neatly half way up along its sides and ends to protect the occupants from mortar and direct fire. The south section of the LZ consisted mainly of the fixed wing landing strip, control tower and some airfield services units.

We were assigned to a tent that was located very close to the revetments on one side and the gate to the adjoining village. The tent area was interesting. Throughout the area there were these mounds of dirt. They were all about the same shape and height, and built solidly of dirt. They had an elevated, circular base to them, with the mound portion going up about three feet or so from the middle of this circle. The dimensions were just right to sit on the base and comfortably lean back on the mound. On the second or the third day there, we found out the mounds were really burial mounds, and we were living in a cemetery. They buried their people sitting up inside the mounds, I think. It didn't stop us from sitting on them.

We were there to get our in country orientation and check rides from the squadron IP. The in-country check out was really neat and a lot different from flight school. We were treated like real pilots, albeit dangerous FNGs, but not like we had been treated before as students. We did a lot of things differently in this training. Rather than doing simulated hydraulics landings and tail rotor failures to the runway, we did them to the rice paddies. The rationale was that we may have other damage to the aircraft, which may necessitate us performing this to the paddies rather than trying to fly them back to some runway. Since we would be working out of rice paddies for the rest of the year it made sense. It also made these maneuvers, very, very tricky.

Each evening a couple of birds would fly back to Two Bits

from Duc Pho where the troop was and RON (remain over night). I think the purpose was to ensure we didn't lose all of our assets in case of an attack on Duc Pho, since they hadn't yet sand-bagged the aircraft's parking places. We got to look forward to these flights for we got to meet some of the guys from the troop, and listen to their stories of the days happening. These guys' stories were amazing . . . and true, we would come to find out.

One night we were outside the tent and I saw a mechanic working on an H-13 scout bird with a Coleman lantern for his only light. I thought to myself "how crazy is this?", and then laughed. In school we had all of these safety signs saying no smoking within 50 feet of the aircraft and this guy has a lantern under the engine changing a fuel pump. Not more than a few minutes later we heard a yell from the mechanic. I looked at the aircraft and saw it fully engulfed in flame. I grabbed my Super 8mm movie camera and recorded the scene on film. I got it on movie film. I knew I wasn't ever gonna get out of this place alive. These guys were certifiably nuts!

Outside the wire was a village. There wasn't much there, ex-cept for the enterprising folks who set up a metal lean-to just beyond the wire fence and set up a couple of barber chairs. One of the male barbers working there had a disfigured leg that he gimped around on. There were also a few young girls who worked there selling cold Coca-Cola to the GIs. The village had an ice plant where you could get ice. The ice was different too. The ice wasn't the rock solid clear ice we know here in the states. Here the ice was more a rigid foggy liquid covered with rice husks. We were warned about drinking non-potable water for fear of con-tracting some of the many diseases present in the population. We had trouble fully complying with the warning. If the water is bad, the ice is bad, and thus the frost and dampness on the Coke bottle would be bad. But when you are thirsty, what the hell.

I never did get sick from anything I ate or drank there. I've felt much worse after downing a dozen White Castles at 1 AM after The Cellar closed on Friday or Saturday night in Brooklyn.

The Cellar was a favorite hangout of ours. Located in the basement of a restaurant and bar out in Bay Ridge, Brooklyn. The place catered to the young 18-20 year old crowd. The music was loud, crowded with standing room only, but the liquor was cheap. There was always a good crowd of people there. Many of them were friends and acquaintances from church or school. The Cellar was a favorite of Tom, Denis, the Jims (Hendren and McKee), and me. We each fell in love there a couple of times I am sure.

Haircuts in Vietnam were a bit different, too. No electricity in the lean to barber shop, meant the barber used hand clippers, scissors, and razors to cut your hair. The haircuts included shaving not only the neck hairs and side burns, but also the hairline of the face and forehead. Following any haircut the barber would give you the mandatory back massage and a neck snap. Boy, the neck snap was exciting the first time they did that to me. I knew I was sitting in a VC chair and wasn't going to make it. I had one barber also crack my ears; just like you crack your knuckles, but with your ears. I still don't know if I liked that at all.

Later in the tour when we returned to LZ Two Bits south, we had a small ground attack one evening. The next morning, they found one of the barbers dead in the concertina wire.

Lastly at the shop outside the gate were the kids. The little orphan-like children who shined boots, and others who were forever looking for a handout. We each sort of adopted a shoeshine boy. I think they really chose us. My shoeshine boy was Choi. (Pronounced like joy with a 'chi' sound for the "j.")

At the gate was where we learned about the culture of VN first hand.

-Three is an unlucky number.

-If you take a picture of 3 boys one will be killed.

-Number 10 is no good, the worst.

-Number 1 is the best.

-Number huckin 1 is the best there is. (They had trouble with the "f" sound.)

We sometimes wanted to walk out towards the fields but the shoeshine boys would not let us, saying that the Viet Cong (VC) were there. Almost like the bogeyman was there. Only we both knew the VC were real. Later whenever we got back to Two Bits overnight we would go see our shoeshine boys, who looked sincerely glad to see we were still alive and glad that we had remembered them.

Though it seemed like a long time, we weren't at Two Bits really that long. We got in country on the 3rd of April, spent probably three nights in Bien Hoa at the Repo depot, and perhaps another four days at An Khe. I don't know when we got to Two Bits, probably about the 10th. But I know we left for and arrived at Duc Pho on the 16th of April 1967.

That day will stay with me a long time. We were to be transported up to Duc Pho to join the Troop. The birds that RON'd the night before brought us up to the Troop. I recall sitting in the back of the Huey facing out the right side of the aircraft. On board were a number of big sacks of mail, and about twenty cases of soda and beer. We flew up at altitude and watched the beautiful South China Sea. I say we went up at altitude, I really mean about 500 feet. That was altitude for us, 500 feet. Anyway, Jim Godfrey, though a gun pilot, was the pilot of the slick going up. I don't know why he flew the slick, I just know that Jim was the pilot that flew me up to the troop that day.

We arrived at Duc Pho and went to see the XO. We were introduced and he asked us who wanted to be scouts, who wanted to be guns, and who wanted to drive slicks. Most all of us raised our hands for the first two, and none for the third choice. He made the determination that Larry Brown and I would go to the slicks and the others would go to guns. He said that if we wanted to, we could transfer to the scouts or guns later. We were pointed to the respective tent area for each of the platoons.

Larry and I went to the Blue lift tent but didn't find anyone there. They were obviously out on a mission. They returned a short time later and said "Hi." We were told to go find a place in the tent. We went in the tent and had trouble seeing. Inside the tent was dark. After my eyes adjusted from the bright sun outside I could see the floors were just dirt. The two main tent poles that supported the center ridgepole of the peak of the tent each had a Coleman lantern hanging from one of the ropes from the tent. I could see that the GP medium was divided into individual areas, which corresponded to the uprights of the tent. Thus there were eight areas. Some of the areas were obviously taken. I could tell because the cots had mosquito nets above them, and there was a sheet of plywood covering the dirt floor adjacent to the cot. On closer look I could also see makeshift desks made out of expended rocket boxes and could see a duffel bag here or there. Larry and I had no difficulty finding a spot, there was plenty of room in the Blue Lift Platoon.

About mid-day we began to sense and feel that something big was going on in the AO (area of operations). The operations tent was hopping and gun and scout teams were coming in and going out. The blues, our organic infantry platoon was on strip alert with the slick platoon. The pilots were hanging very close to the cockpits awaiting the signal to "launch the Blues." Being new guys you weren't in the communication loop and everybody was too busy to stop and explain things to you. And as new guys you didn't want to appear too stupid by asking stupid questions. You just hung out and observed and tried to figure out for yourself some sense of what is happening.

Larry and I went down to the flight line just in time to see one of the gun birds come back in with only one pilot. We learned that the pilot had been hit in the vicinity of Jim Godfrey's crash. Jim had be hit and crashed. 16 April 1967. That's the day I joined B 1/9 CAV at Duc Pho. I think a captain also was killed that day, but in another aircraft.

Welcome to B Troop Mister John Flanagan;
   and Mister Larry Brown,;
    and Mister Griff Bedworth;
     and Mister Dave Bressam;
      and Mister Terry Connor.

Chapter Nine

Welcome to the Blue Lift

The cavalry troop was divided into three platoons. scout, gun and lift platoon. Scouts were the "white" birds and flew in little OH 13 observation helicopters with one pilot and one observer / gunner. Guns were the "red" birds and flew B and C model Hueys with two pilots, a crew chief (CE) and a door gunner. The lift section was the "blue" platoon and flew D model Hueys with two pilots, and a crew chief. The lift section also carried the Blues, our organic—and absolutely heroic!!—platoon of infantry.

The troop had 10 scout birds, 10 gun birds, four lift ships or slicks, and a maintenance ship. The maintenance bird was the same type as the lift birds and we would use it when one of our birds was in for maintenance, turned in, or awaiting replacement. We also used this bird in the lift platoon when we had enough pilots to fly it.

The scout birds were armed usually with a 7.62 mm skid gun on the left side and a scout observer who was armed with an M60 and an enormous supply and variety of grenades. The grenades included the white phosphorous or "Willy Peter." Willy Peter was great for burning hooches and clearing out bunkers and spider holes. Fragmentation grenades helped with servicing those targets as well. The remaining grenades were different colors and used to mark locations. Mostly the smokes were used to mark enemy locations and areas for the gunships to target. A couple of scouts had 3 rockets on the right side to augment their weapons. The gunships had an array of weapons systems. Bobby Zahn had the hog. A Huey armed with 48 rockets. He could put a rocket through a small window if you needed it. Another was the Frog that had a 40mm grenade launcher mounted in a nose turret, and carried 14 rockets, 7 on each side. Another had 2 seven round rocket pods above which were mounted twin 7.62 machine guns. The gunships also had a crewchief and a door gunner each armed with the M60 on a bungee cord. They, like the scout observers, had an array of grenades as well.

Lift ships were referred to as "slicks" because unlike the other birds in the troop we didn't carry any guns. Well, each crewchief had a 7.62mm M60 machine gun suspended from a bungee cord. Although they had the M-60 for suppressive and point targeting, they never fired it much. They were too busy keeping us clear of other aircraft and tree stumps and paddy dikes during landing, as well as passing on information and taking care of the blues in the back. On takeoff from the LZs the crew chiefs would hold onto the upper track of the door jam and stand outside the aircraft looking above and to the rear of the aircraft to keep us clear of climbing into another aircraft over flying us.

The First of the Ninth Way In normal air cavalry operations the scouts and the guns went on reconnaissance flights to find the enemy or areas of likely enemy activity. We would develop the area by inserting the Blues on the ground and would sweep the area and bring the reconnaissance to the enemy. Their job was to go into the village and the huts, and the tunnels and find the enemy. Once found, they would have to maintain contact with them. Once contact with the bad guys was established the red and white birds would help maintain contact and cover the Blues. The guns and scouts would also try to contain the enemy so they couldn't escape while the lift went back to pick up the ready reaction force (RRF). The ready reaction force was a normal infantry unit that would be assigned a mission to standby to support our Blues if they found something and needed help. They would wait at the pick-up point until we would show up and airlift them in to the fight. We were then supposed to pull the Blues out and let the normal infantry fight it out, while we went looking for more bad guys. That was the theory. In reality our Blues would start the fight and stay there until the fighting had ended, regardless of how many infantry units we had to put in to help them.

Being a lift pilot was different from the other platoons and different from the flying we did in flight school. The scouts and the guns went out as armed teams looking for the bad guy. Once they identified the bad guys, they could kill them. Of course, if the bad guys saw them first, or the good guys didn't get all of the bad guys on the first pass then a good-old shoot out would take place. The important part to understand as we contrast the red and white platoons with the Blue section was they—the guns and scouts-were flying over the area pouring out death and destruction on the enemy below, while we were taxiing folks in and out of the rice paddies.

Lest I mislead you, the guns and scouts would sometimes almost have to hover in front of the bad guys in order to deliver accurate and decisive fires. When the lift was landing or the Blues were in contact, I have seen guns and scouts fly back and forth over a tree line or trenches peddle turning at each end to maximize the amount of time their guns were on the bad guys.

The lift platoon was virtually unarmed. In reality, the guns and the scouts were always working so close to us we didn't need the crewchief's firepower. When we came into an area our purpose was to put the Blues on the ground, and the most important thing that crew chief could do was make sure we didn't stick our tails into the ground on landing or on take off climb into another aircraft above us. That means you not only have to slow down, you have to stop too. The bad guys also know where you are going because the guns had probably prepped the LZ (landing zone) with their on-board rockets. Or in the case of planned assaults, the prep would be performed by 105, 155 or 175mm artillery, backed up with 2.75 rockets and machine gunfire from the guns.

So lift pilots flew out and landed in front of the bad guys who knew beforehand where we were coming to and when. Our crew chiefs would be hanging out of the aircraft on approach watching for wires and making sure the tail rotor didn't come in contact with anything. On take off the crewchief would be standing on the floor with his body out of the cabin clearing the sky to the rear and the above to ensure we didn't run into another bird. They readied the bird in the morning before the pilot's preflight and flew along on the missions. They went on the ground to load and unload the troops, equipment, wounded and dead. And they pulled maintenance when we weren't flying. Then at the end of the day when the pilot's left for the night, they did the paperwork and pulled the daily maintenance. I have a lot of respect for these guys. The crewchief is really the unsung hero in army aviation. And ours were the best—Earl Hobbs (Lubbock, Texas), Art Dunn, Dale Dungan (Colorado), "Tank"Tankersley (Nicetooth, Arkansas), Billy Schutt (Boraga, Michigan), Silas Sims, Berken, and all the others whose names have passed with time. In the other platoons, and other units the crew chiefs also had a door gunner to help them maintaining the aircraft; in Blue Lift we only had the crew chief.

In order to minimize the exposure time available for the bad guy to get us, and to maximize the fire power of the blue platoon we had to get them in as close to each other as possible in terms of both time and space.

In order to do this we always flew close formations. The best formation for the Blues was a four-ship diamond, which allowed us all to hit the LZ at the same time and deploy the Blues in a tactical platoon formation. Other formations we used were: trail—

where we lined up one behind the other; staggered trail—where every other aircraft would offset to the right of the trail formation; echelon right or left—where we were diagonally offset to one side or the other, and finally the line. We would only go in on line to an LZ when we were going in to ridgelines. The most frequent formation was the diamond.

Formations:

```
  X        X        X           X         X X X X X
 X X       X        X           X
  X        X        X           X
           X        X           X
Diamond   Trail  Staggered Trail  Echelon Right  Right Line
```

When you flew formation you really didn't look to see where you were going, you just fixed the position of the other aircraft on your windshield and kept him there. By this I mean you reacted to every move he did. It's amazing, you really don't realize all the information you are getting from looking at the other aircraft; any slight movement of the other aircraft and you would instantly become aware of it and react. In formation you fly with very minute pressures from your fingers on the controls. "Just think about moving the control," we used to tell the new guys, just think about it and the aircraft will do what you want. Tighten up and move the controls a lot, and you were in for the ride of your life. You cannot physically react to the aircraft quick enough you had to "think" it through. And the thinking soon became instinctive.

Blue flight as seen from Saber Blue 39's position in
the rear of the formation as we begin our descent to
pick up the Blues. Photo courtesy of Jim Pratt

Blue flight begins a steep approach to the PZ.
Photo courtesy of Jim Pratt

The Blues come into sight. Each squad of Blues has
one squad member stand facing the final approach
course with their weapon held above their head
indicating where each slick should touchdown. Photo
courtesy of Jim Pratt

Just before touch down in the PZ. Photo courtesy of
Jim Pratt

Flying formation was fun. We used to fly particularly close
sometimes to let the Blues take pictures of each other. Of course
the pilots did a lot of picture taking as well. I also remember
seeing pictures of mid-air "full moons" and "pressed hams" being shot from one aircraft to another. You haven't seen a moon,
until you've seen one at 500 feet over the rice paddies of Vietnam.

To minimize the time spent in the LZ we didn't really land in
the LZ. As we turned on to final approach the Blues would lower
themselves from the seats and sit on the floor. Then as we got
closer to the approach they would grip the underside of the seats
and step out onto the skids. As we slowed and arrived in the LZ,
and between 3—5 feet in the air, the Blues would all jump. They
tried to time it so that one side would jump at a time. In the
cockpit the loss of this much weight from one side, then the other,
rocked the aircraft violently, unless you were anticipating the
weight shift. Then as soon as one went the other side did the
same thing and the pilot has to correct for it. The crew chief

would check to make sure they were all off and tell us we were up. And off we would go on the takeoff. During takeoff and initial climb the crewchief would either hangout or stand up outside the cabin ensuring we were clear above, and would not run into another aircraft.

Crewchiefs can be seen standing outside the cabin as
we hover to take off from Duc Pho

While it's fun flying formation, it ain't easy learning to fly close formation. And there is a big difference between flying an empty helicopter and one that is loaded; especially when touching down during a combat assault in an LZ. On the first combat assault I actually had the controls for, just south of Duc Pho, the aircraft commander told me to make the approach to the ground. That is, rather than terminating at a hover like we did the most of the time in school, he wanted me to fly it straight to the ground. I did, and I pranged the bird and spread the skids a bit. Not enough to cause any serious damage, but enough to give the bird a rather rakish look to it as it sat there slung just a little lower than the rest. The AC, the good Lieutenant—Chandler, Pete Chandler, I think his name was—was too short to really say anything about it. I have to say that I would have been all right but I got into one of the other bird's downwash and just continued to the ground a bit quicker than I had expected. I would have been okay had I terminated to a hover, but he was on me to take it to the ground. So I did! Good thing the paddy was still a bit wet, as the mud had cushioned the landing (impact?) a bit.

The Huey D model was an extension of the earlier Hueys. The D model provided a larger cabin area to accept more troops and had a larger engine. There were 11 seats in the back and two in the front for the pilots. Of course the daytime temperature was so damn hot over there, and the density altitude so high, you couldn't take off with full fuel and a full load of troops. The arrangement of troop seats in the D models was very flexible. Most units used a forward facing bench arrangement with the transmission coves reserved for the crew chief and the door gunner. Two of the single seats were positioned behind the pilots' seats. The crew chiefs in most of the slick assault companies had machine gun mounts attached to the aircraft and positioned in front of the seats in the transmission coves. We didn't use them because they were too heavy and we only had the crew chief.

B Troop, (and I think the other troops in the squadron) was different. First, we didn't have a door gunner, nor did we have the heavy external mounts for the M60 door guns. Second, our troop seats were set up to face outwards. This left one seat right in front of the transmission that was blocked by the two rows of out-facing seats. Our crewchief always rode behind the pilots (AC or P in the figure below) and had his machine gun on a bungee cord suspended from the doorframe. The side the crew chief flew on was dependent on which ship in the formation he was in. I was Three-seven (Saber Blue 37), and flew the left wing in the diamond; my crew chief was on the left side behind my seat; Three-six flew the right wing, his crew chief was on the right, etc.

Jim Pratt (L) and John Flanagan alongside Jim's UH-
1D aircraft.
Note the seats are facing outward for quick boarding
and exiting.

We gave up fuel for troops. Instead of taking on 1200 pounds
of fuel, we would start with only 800 lbs. This reduced our available flight time from 2:15 minutes to something much less. This
was not a problem most of the time since we were rarely more
than 10 minutes from the action. And we could typically drop
the Blues, get the reaction force and insert them before we had to
get more fuel. Some days it didn't happen that way, but most of
the time it did.

Most of the days we kept track of flight time on the windshield in grease pencil. It would normally be a series of ten to
twenty minute flights. We didn't get a lot of flight time in the
slicks, but we had lots of intense takeoffs and landings during
the time we were out. Most of the helicopter pilots came back
from Vietnam boasting 1000 hours of combat flight time; we were
lucky to log 700—800 hours. Maybe not a lot of hours, but they
were intense hours, I can assure you.

Laager Areas Our tactics allowed us to get away with reduc-
ing fuel loads most of the time. Rather than reacting to the battle
from our base, we would operate out of forward laager areas.
Laager areas could be anywhere from a regular airfield, an es-

tablished LZ, or a section of paddy, rural road or soccer field that we just took over and landed on. There was many a day the tactics didn't apply, and we each would land well into the 20-minute fuel warning light. I know of no one in B Troop during my time that actually ran out of fuel in the field, however.

I don't know the steps I had to go through or the length of time it took, but it didn't take long before I was in and tight on the formation and could really make that D model sing. At some time you became one with the machine. Your body takes on the dimensions of the aircraft. Your shoulders become 48 foot wide, the same length as the rotor from tip to tip. And just as you know without thinking that you can walk through a doorway without bumping your shoulders, you know if you can fit in an LZ or how close you can get to the other aircraft in formation.

I didn't really realize how tight, tight was in formation flying until I went back to a tactical helicopter unit in Korea in 1980 as the battalion executive office. There in my first couple of weeks with the unit I was back flying in formation. When I got the old familiar sight picture of the ship in front-that is, when I framed the other helicopter in the windshield like I remembered it back in B Troop—I knew we were about to mesh rotors. Boy, it must have been tight. I know, "the older I get the better I was" goes the old saying, but not really in this case; the guys have enough pictures—before zoom lenses by the way—that show the closeness of our formations.

It wasn't all flying The troop had not been at Duc Pho for long before I joined up with them. Although the landing areas for the platoons had been scraped flat and covered with perma prime the aircraft parking spots had not been revetted. Perma prime was an oily based black tar-ish kind of a liquid that was sprayed over the ground and over time it would harden. Sometimes it took a lot of time to harden, given the high ambient temperatures for most of the year. When they perma primed our area at Duc Pho it would cake on the soles of your boots. Since flying a helicopter demands you make endless small corrections to the pedals by constantly pressing and releasing the pedals, the addition of the perma prime caused your boots to hang up frequently. This would require gross movements of the feet and legs, causing somewhat erratic actions of the aircraft. This did not help your pilot technique or in trying to have a light touch on the controls. Luckily no one got hurt because of this. I did feel sorry for the crew chief that had to bust his butt to clean the mess from the helicopter floors and controls. And remember the Blues had the same stuff on the bottom of their boots as well! The aircraft were really a mess during these times, no matter how careful you tried to be.

Revetments are sandbag walls arranged around the aircraft to protect them from grazing fires and close hitting mortar and rocket fire. Revetments came in a variety of styles and construction. In the rear area, such as the "Golf Course" at An Khe the revetments were three-sided "U" shaped and constructed professionally by the Army engineers. The walls of the revetment were made of PSP or metal planks on either side of a sandbag wall. We also used wooden ammo boxes from the gunships' the rockets, and empty 55-gallon drums in place of actual sandbags. We would fill the boxes or barrels with sand and use them as walls. Once filled the boxes would stack pretty well. The revetments were about 4 or 5 feet tall, as I recall.

At some places the revetments took the form of an "L" shape. This made hovering in and out of the spot a bit easier. At Duc Pho our platoon's area necessitated us parking close to and parallel to the slope of a hill. The parking spots were one behind the other. The revetments we built here consisted of single sandbag walls parallel to the hillside.

There wasn't much room between these revetments at Duc Pho, and there were no markings to tell you how far forward or rearward you were. So positioning the aircraft in its optimal spot was difficult. If you were coming in off a single ship mission and the guy in the parking spot behind you was a bit too far forward, you would have to go to the front of your spot and back in. No-where in school, or anyplace else did they teach you how to parallel park a Huey. Let me tell you, it is an experience to re-member, but you got quite proficient at it in no time.

Revetments caused many a problem for the pilots. Despite being warned not to takeoff directly over the front wall of the "U" shaped revetments, many a pilot did and suffered the conse-quences of hooking a skid, rolling over and crashing immediately. Many a crewmember was killed doing this.

At Duc Pho I learned that being a CAV pilot was not only about flying. Being a CAV pilot was also about a lot of manual labor. Up where we were there were no engineers to build the revetments. We did it ourselves. Commissioned and warrant of-ficer pilots, enlisted crew chiefs and our Blues working side by side filling sand bags between combat assaults. Life in the CAV was going to be different.

We did other things besides performing manual labor. There was a lot of hanging out waiting for something to do. We played a lot of chess and played a lot of hearts. At the laager sites we would have a continuous round of hearts going on. Hands were taken over by pilots coming in off missions in place of guys pre-paring to launch. "Hours and hours of shear boredom, punctuated by moments of shear terror," is how helicopter flying is often described. The description can be equally applied to life in B Troop. One moment you could be playing your tenth hand of hearts and in the midst of running the deck when the speaker would blast "Launch Blue!" The next moment you would be rac-ing to the site of a downed bird with a hot gunfight going on, and you had to land in the center of it. "Never a backwards glance, nor a moments hesitation, Drive on, goddamnit, Drive on!" I can hear the encouragement from Bert Chole (Saber White and later Saber 3) as B Troop went about doing what we did best.

27 May 1967, Duc Pho The morning of 27 May was like most of the rest of the days since arriving in B Troop. I had settled down and was flying as Three-nine x-ray. Callsign numbers are spoken as individual single digit numbers. For example Jim's callsign was Saber Blue 39 and spoken as Saber BlueThree-nine. WO1 Jim Pratt the aircraft commander for 39 and flew in the "slot" or last ship in the formation. I was Jim's peter pilot/ co-pilot and referred to as his "X-ray," both terms of endearment for the junior of the two pilots. We flew together on a daily basis and became quite good friends and an exceptional flight crew. We went though a lot together.

Author WO1 John Flanagan Duc Pho 1967
Every officer, including Warrant Officers, wore the
Cavalry Crossed Sabers. Bush hats with colored
material identified officers of the Red, White, and
Blue Platoons. (Guns, Scouts, and Lift Platoons)

On this day we had been doing a series of village sweeps with the Blues north of Duc Pho. We would make a combat assault to one end of the village dropping the Blues off. They would sweep the village and we would pick them up at the PZ (pick-up zone) at the other end of the village. Along the way they would blow some bunkers, have some minor shoot outs, and perhaps burn a hooch or two when the occupants wouldn't come out, and a CS smoke, or fragmentation grenade would set the hooch on fire. We did this all morning. In and out, in and out, refuel, in and out. Sometimes they would bring out some detainee (prisoner) for questioning and we would haul them back to the compound, and then rejoin the lift.

This day right before lunchtime we had just picked the Blues up from what seemed to be, the umpteenth village. We were all ready for some chow, and the Blues settled in for the ride home. Enroute we got a call from OPs saying that "Higher wants you to put the Blues in at some set of military grid coordinates indicating a place on the map. They have a report of a regimental CP in the vicinity."

Yeah right. Well the scouts and the guns go over and select an LZ for us and cover us on the approach. The LZ selected was a tiny two ship LZ. Mac McAnally Blue 38, and us Blue 39 stretched it out on final to allow enough room for 35 and 36 to get in, drop their guys and begin their take off before we came into the LZ. No sweat. We dropped the Blues and joined up with 35 and 36. Shortly after, the radio came alive signaling the Blues were in heavy contact and had taken some casualties. Blue flight headed to pick up the ready reaction force as the Blues fought heroically to secure the casualities and get an LZ ready for us to insert the RRF and pick up the wounded. The radios were alive with gun birds and scouts talking to each other, coordinating their gun runs over the Blues. The Blues were reporting taking fire from 360 degrees around their positions as we did this. The Blues were in trouble and they had wounded. We needed to get reinforcements into them and get our wounded out.

Scout pilot Jere Anderson—also known as Fat Albert—told me years later that he was the first scout over the village when we were diverted to check the area. He said that he was coming off another mission and had just very few M60 ammunition left onboard when he arrived over the ville. He said he knew it looked bad. He didn't see any dogs, or chickens or people there. It looked bad, real bad. Since he had so little ammunition he had decided to save it in case he was shot down.

We went to pick up the ready reaction force that was standing on strip alert. Luckily for us, the pick up point was just a short distance between Duc Pho and the site of the fight. We picked up the reaction force and returned to the area. We were put in a holding pattern until Saber 6 could get the situation sorted out and made sure we could get in there for the Blues. As we orbited and orbited, the guns and the scout teams were covering the Blues and trying to gain control so we could drop the reaction force in the same paddies as the Blues. As the time passed, we begin to monitor the fuel remaining a little more closely. The entire flight was getting low. We did everything we could to conserve fuel. Slowed down to best cruise, also beeped the rpm back about 6200 rpm to conserve fuel. There was a continuing discussion as to whether this really saved any fuel. I still don't know—but we did it all the same. As we got close to coming out of orbit, Blue 35, Captain Don Burnham our platoon leader and AC of the lead ship had us report fuel status. Jim and I were the lowest on fuel. Being the tail end Charlie fighting dirty air on landing and takeoff always costs more fuel than the others do who had clean air. We were really concerned about be able to make the approach and getting back without running out of fuel. The situation was made particularly more intense because someone had scratched in the instrument panel alongside the fuel gauge "Engine quits @ 150 Pounds of Fuel."

Because of our fuel status, 35 told us to move up in the formation and take 36's position. This put us in the first flight of two behind 35, and put 36 back in our place. We were finally given the green light to break the pattern and begin the approach. 35, 39 first; then 38 and 36 bringing up the rear. The gunships were tucked in close to us and provided a base of fire as we slowed to touch down in the LZ.

We knew that 35 was going to wait in the LZ to pick up one of our Blues who got wounded during the interim period. Guzzi was from New Jersey, I think he had gotten hit that day. Because of the tight space of the LZ, we would wait with 35 until he got him aboard.

We went in, waited and got out with no problem. There was firing coming up from everywhere, but no hits. Jim and I broke off of 35, began a climb and headed directly to the POL point. We climbed to altitude just in case we were going to lose the engine we figured we had a better chance of autorotating successfully from altitude. We requested a straight in approach with no delay, direct to the POL pad. The Duc Pho tower cleared us. We shot an approach to the ground, landing on the pad. We throttled the engine back as the crew chief began refueling. We believe the engine quit, or at least was on the verge of quitting as the crew chief began the refueling.

Although we had no problem that doesn't mean everyone was happy. As we were leaving the LZ, we could hear 38 and 36 coming in right behind us. The fire intensified as we made our way on the climb. As 38 and 36 came out, 36 reported receiving hits, and finally saying "I'm going down." We couldn't do anything because of our fuel status.

The guns provided cover for the downed crew, as the Blues moved to secure the aircraft and crew. The nature of our operations always leads to voids in memory of what really happened. This is due mainly to the fact that, although involved in the same action, we were involved in different pieces of it with different individual concerns. For example, the Blues didn't know about our fuel status, and we weren't aware of their individual ground battle. Neither of us were aware of Jere Anderson's plight. It is not until 34 years later when you listen to the others or read their accounts told in a variety of books that you get a fuller picture of what went on. There are, after all of these years, striking differences in recollections. Fat Albert said that he found a few NVA hiding in a spider hole and had to ask Saber Six to come over and kill these guys for him.

I don't know how Mac got out. Mac still blames me and Jim for getting him shot down. Remember that if the formation had stayed intact, Jim and I would have been at the tail end, not Mac.

Jim and I did real well. We never received a hit the entire time we flew together. Yet all of the other ships were hit and many shot down. Mac seemed to attract hits. We began referring to him as "magnate ass."

As we were refueling, 35 came in and took the refueling pad ahead of us. As the crew chief was putting the fuel in we could see it run out the bottom as if to come out of a sprinkler. We called him and advised him of his situation. 35 left POL and hopped the rise to our landing area. So at the end of the 2nd lift in to the "suspected regimental CP" B Troop's lift capability was down to Blue 38 and 39. 35 was battle damaged and safe at home, and 36 was down in the rice paddy.

With 35 and 36 out of action, the rest of the day was very busy for 38 and 39. We made a couple of more lifts in to the area. And we continued to shuttle ammo, and supplies in to the Blues. We were also called in to direct other friendly mounted ground units into the area.

The fight went on. Just prior to darkness we went in and brought in ammo for the night. The guns stayed out all night over the Blues. We stayed ready to launch to render any assistance we could. As the other friendlies fought their way in towards the Blues there was some argument concerning who killed which bad guy. The Blues didn't like folks taking credit for their kills. To solve the problem the Blues would kill a bad guy and then go out and drag his body inside their "perimeter." That's what I was told by some of the Blues shortly after the fight. My flight log shows that we put in about four and half hours of flight time that day and logged 11 landings. 4.5 hours isn't a lot of time for helicopters in Vietnam. But for Blue Lift it is a lot considering the distance from Duc Pho to the fight scene was less than 10 minutes.

The next morning I flew in to re-supply the Blues and there neatly lined up were about 30 bodies. A couple of Blues were sitting very close by eating their 'Cs' for breakfast. For the action on May 27th, many in the unit were recommended for awards. Jim and I were among those who received the Distinguished Flying Cross for heroism. The awards were presented to us by the 1st Cavalry Division Commanding General, Major General John Tolson. Upon hearing that I had received the Distinguished Flying Cross my brother Dave sent me the history of the medal which he had researched in the library. I didn't know much about the medal until Dave sent me the article.

Life in Blue Lift I enjoyed the Blue Lift section. We were a close bunch of guys for the most part. The core of the lift section for most of the year were Jim Pratt, Loren McAnally, Tom "Wonder Warthog" Maehrlein, Mike Covey, Nubbs Hirning, and me. There was also at the beginning LT Chandler, Don Lewis, CPT Don Burnham who later was KIA in a crash while on a GCA into Da Nang, and CPT Ivan "Sky King" Camp. Others came through the lift section and went to guns or scouts. Larry Brown, Gary Hanna (KIA during Tet, days after leaving the Blues), Larry Kreps. Others came in towards the last half of the tour. Jack Craft, Zorba the Greek, LT Walls. And I am sure lots of others, to whom I apologize for forgetting to mention them by name. I had planned on transferring to the scouts or the guns after awhile, but got to know the guys in Blue Lift and decided to stay. I don't think I made a mistake.

The pilots of Blue Lift 1967 In front of "Darlin' Jenny"
Back row: Don Burnham, Ivan Camp, Jim Pratt, Larry
Kreps, Larry Brown
Front: Tom Maehrlein, Mike Covey, John Flanagan,
Don Lewis

I enjoyed working for the Blues. I always tried to make life a little easier and better for them. On approach to the LZs I tried to get them to a dry rice paddy, or at least put them close to the protection of a dyke. Or at least close so they wouldn't have any extra trudging through the paddies. I always carried extra cartoons of cigarettes and candy on board for them, as well as a box of C4 explosives, just in case they need it.

We lived in tents most of the time. Our tents were right next to the Blues, the enlisted infantrymen who were our original frequent flyers. Between the tents we would gather in our folding beach chairs and pass the time. Stories were told about wine, women and home. Things we were going to do when we got back to the Land of the Big PX. We talked about and traded stories of the day's fight, and of previous fights. The time spent together served to bond us closer together. I think this made us a better unit overall. We cared about each other. And we knew it. We also knew the CAV sucks. We could say it, because we were in the CAV. You can't say it cause you ain't. Our daily deeds contributed to building quite a reputation among the Army. "If you ain't CAV, you ain't shit" is the slogan. And if you ain't in the 9th CAV you ain't in the "Real CAV." (Of course non-cavalry guys would go on and say, "if you are Cav, you are shit." That's usually when the fighting would start.)

James G. Pratt We passed the time in lots of different ways. Jim Pratt had to indoctrinate every new pilot and many a new Blue with his tall and lengthy tale of the Fu Bird. If you haven't heard it, ask Jim about it, but please make sure I'm not around. I can't take anymore of it. Jim told me the story one-day when we were flying from Duc Pho to An Khe to Plieku to Kontum and then back along the same route. He began the story as we lifted off of Duc Pho and finished it as the blades slowly came to a stop some nine or ten hours later. I could have killed him. Many a person who has been subjected to this story in the intervening years, I am sure, wish that I had killed them and spared them the ordeal.

Jim also played the harmonica (badly), guitar (badly) and sang (badly) little ditties he had made up. They ditties were pretty good. Of course compared to his playing and voice, the ingredients on the side of a frozen TV dinner would sound good.

I had a great time flying with Jim. We did some pretty dumb things, but they were fun. One of our single ship flights was from Duc Pho to Kontum to re-supply and bring mail to a pink team we had supporting another unit. Jim and I flew the entire way from An Khe to Kontum low level over the road. We tried to see if we could stay exactly over the road and make the turns at ninety knots instead of the highway speed of 45 or so. There were few turns we missed, but not many. During one leg we came upon a convoy of trucks. Jim and I began talking about the difficulty of landing in the bed of the truck. How tough could it be? So we lined up and shot an approach to the back of a two and half ton truck. We got the skids inside the uprights of the truck before pulling up. We were afraid one of the couple or three soldiers in the back of the truck may try to jump on the skids. All I know is a couple of soldiers got some great close up pictures of the Huey.

On one mission to Kontum we were to RON and chase Larry Brown back the next day. He was going to bring back an H-13 scout bird to An Khe. Jim and I had nothing to do once we got there so we headed off to the village. We found a couple of little places where they had cokes and beer. The beer was real good. We realized we had stayed too long when we looked outside to find the country had gone pitch black. Rather than risk being out in the night with both friendly and bad guy patrols we stayed where we were and drank some more beer. We woke up the next morning and walked back to the compound. I have no memory of what went on that night. Someone was looking out for us I know. We were lucky to stay in the right hooch, on the right night.

The flight back was uneventful. We chased Larry in his little H-13 scout bird as he flew low level adjacent to the highway. It took us longer to get back because of the low top speed of the H13 compared to the Huey. The time did give us an opportunity as we flew through the Mang Yang pass to reflect on the great French battle that was fought there, and to salute the heroic French dead who are buried on the sides of the pass.

Larry Brown is a fearless guy who I treasure as a close friend and confidant. Larry was born in Pensacola Florida and raised in a Navy family. He lived most of his life on the West Coast and the Pacific. He attended college for a while but dropped out to join the Army and fly helicopters. Larry's about a year and half older than me. We flew slicks together until he went to the Scouts. Larry Brown became White 14 and earned the title of Super Scout. This title bestowed on him by one of our greatest B Troop Commander Major George Burrows. On our first tour, Larry was credited with over 150 enemy kills. Though Larry was shot down seven times.

Larry received a commission to armor and returned to Vietnam. On his second tour he stopped counting at 117. On this tour Larry met an Army nurse and they fell in love. They were married in Vietnam. Larry ultimately transferred to the army reserves where he retired as a lieutenant colonel. His wife Carol is a Colonel in the reserves and is an Army War College graduate. They are a great team of Americans.

Movies Each evening just as it got dark, the entire troop would police up their beach chairs and go over to the area beside the Operations Tent and watch a movie projected onto some sheets hung by rope between two tents. There weren't many movies on the circuit, so we got to see some of them very often. The lift pilots, instigated by Pratt formed a plot one evening. The lift pilots all went up to the movie as usual and arranged their chairs side by side in one neat row stretching the breadth of the small seating area. Jim Pratt took the aisle seat on the right, facing the screen. I was next, then Mac and Covey, then Warthog, and so on. About halfway through the movie, Jim sprang to his feet, grabbed his chair, and shouted "Holy shit!" and pointed towards the ground as he backed away. I followed instantly, jumping up and yelling, "Look at the size of that thing!" as I pointed to the thing moving across the ground. The others followed suit, yelling in turn such things as 'Watch out for the teeth," Look at the tail," and others. Before Wonder had gotten completely to his feet, the entire troop was up and clearing the area. A quick check determined the area was clear of the thing, and everyone was trying to figure out what they had just seen. After a while we all sat down and watched the rest of the movie. No one else was the wiser about our intruder. Though we had a pretty hard time sitting there without laughing out loud.

Jim was real good at role-playing. He had that kind of Don Knotts quality to him, and he was always ready to go to the extreme for a joke. We got in a couple of new guys, and we decided to play a prank on them. We developed a story about Pratt seeing so much action that it had affected him a lot. To the point that we believed Jim was dangerous. Jim played the role by always sharpening his knife and talking sweetly to it. He sandbagged his bunk, and would hide behind pretending to shoot the bad guys.

He would make quick sharp slashing and stabbing movements with the knife, and talk to himself out loud. He would alternately clean his sidearm instead of sharpening the knife. Jim wouldn't go anywhere without his helmet and a bandoleer of linked ammunition. Jim was really scary. In the middle of the night Jim would make sure the new guy would see him creep about the tent. Watching the new guys reactions to Jim's antics was absolutely hysterical. Just watching Jim was funny. Watching the reactions of the others made it even more hysterical. Sometimes you wondered if this was not, perhaps the real Jim Pratt? Jim was originally from Brocton Massachusetts, a small town on the south side of Boston. He was about five months older than I was, but more importantly he had graduated from flight school and arrived in B Troop about two months before me. That made him the more experienced guy and the aircraft commander. I was his willing student as I learned the ropes from Jim.

Practical joking stays a part of the B Troopers even today after 32 years. At a reunion of the Bullwhip Squadron Association, a production company (Arrowhead Productions, Austin, Texas) interviewed Jim, Barry Mc Alpine, and me. They were filming footage for a planned big screen movie. As Jim and I were being interviewed I spied Larry Brown sheepishly walking alongside the inside wall of the museum. As he approached a place close to the corner of the wall he surveyed the area to make sure he was mostly hidden from everyone's sight. That is, except mine and the rest of our group who were looking at the interview from behind my location. Convinced he was okay, Larry turned around, bent over and shot us a full moon. I tried as hard as I could but when I looked at Jim's face I knew he knew and I just burst out laughing. I felt sorry for the poor director. Here was Barry telling about dragging one of the Blues bodies back through the rice paddy and Jim and I burst out laughing. When we told him what had happened, he said why didn't you tell me, I would have swung the camera around! In any case the humor kept us on our toes and provided an avenue for some emotional release.

Wonder Warthog Wonder Warthog, also known as Tom Maehrlein, was a singular circumstance as well. The Troop had an SOP that you didn't go anywhere without your sidearm and helmet. Tom referred to these as his army gun and hard hat. Tom had gotten chewed out a couple times by CPT Burnham for going to the head or shower without his army gun and hard hat. Tom learned and complied; but on his own terms. Often you would see Tom enroute to the shower dressed only in his army gun, carrying his towel and soap in his hard hat.

Tom was and still is today certifiably crazy. He had no sense of fear or apprehension at all. Tom, or Wonder Warthog as he preferred to be called, believed he was invincible, and this gave him a big pair of balls. He truly deserved the Medal of Honor for his rescue of two crewmembers of B Troop who had been a part of a four-man crew shot down near the Citadel at Hue during the Tet Offensive of 1968. The weather was bad and the ceilings were low. Tom was flying with someone from squadron on an ash and trash run when he flew over a rice paddy when he spotted a Huey sitting in the middle of the paddy. There were two groups of dinks as Tom described it. Each group had taken two crewmen prisoner. Tom immediately shot an approach under intense small arms fire to one group in the paddy. The dinks ran away from the helicopter and the two crewmen scrambled aboard. Unfortunately, the other group executed the other crewmembers before Tom could get them. Neither intense ground fire, nor being outnumbered and alone discouraged him from taking immediate action. I believe that is conspicuous valor of the highest order, and deserved more than the Distinguished Service Cross he received.

Flying Pots Some things that happened weren't really funny, but they were. For instance one afternoon Captain Lewis was walking back to the tents from the flight line by way of the maintenance area. The maintenance area was at the north end of the lift section's parking area. Beyond the maintenance area was the tent area for the Blues and the Blue Lift pilots. The maintenance team was running up a Huey there to track the main rotor blades.

Tracking referred to the path the individual blades pass through the air. If they were in track they would pass at about the same position relative to the air and you had a smooth ride. If, on the other hand the blades were out of track the aircraft would bounce on each rotation of the blades. The bigger the difference, the bigger the bounce, the bigger the bounce the less comfortable you were, and less efficient the aircraft was. In order to track the blades they would color the tips of the blades. With the aircraft run up to operating RPMs they would load the (increase the pitch) rotor system. A mechanic with some tape stretched between two long horizontal brackets extending from a long pole would attempt to carefully move the pole so as to position the vertical tape in a position to come in gentle contract with the tips of the blades. Then they would compare the cuts of the tape and make adjustments to the blades. Then they would try it again, until the blades cut through the same place on the tape.

The area was getting quite windy and dusty as the maintenance test pilot increased pitch as Captain Lewis approached the area. Of course increasing pitch increased the downdraft from the spinning main rotor. So much so, that a cloud of dust began to grow larger accompanied by some small debris. Thinking quickly, Lewis sought cover and protection behind the two-hole shitter next to the maintenance area. The test pilot loaded the blades so much that the shit house became airborne and blew over on top of Lewis. Lewis was trapped momentarily under the weight of the shithouse. We all came running and someone called for the medics. Our medic came and put Lewis on a stretcher. The jeep showed up and we laid the stretcher across the hood of the jeep and we rushed him up to the aid tent. We later told him we had put him in for the Purple Heart, and even gave him a draft copy of the citation. We also put up a sign for all to see declaring the shitter as the "Captain Lewis Memorial Shitter."

Jim Pratt related to me that when he was going through the CH-47 transition course on the way back to Vietnam for his second tour that he ran into CPT Lewis at the club. Lewis upon seeing him got up and came over to Jim and said "Pratt, if you ever tell these guys about the shit house I'll kill you!" Jim said he kept his mouth shut since he was a student status and Lewis was an instructor pilot.

Honey Pots One time a few weeks after this incident we had a couple of US Navy officers come visit us for a closer look at the countryside. These guys ran the LST type boats up and down the coast. Jim and I had picked them up on the beach by LZ Montezuma an ammunition supply depot on the South China Sea. As I was walking up the flight line with them I saw that they were having an animated conversation between themselves and directing their attention towards the Don Lewis Memorial Shitter. I asked if there was something wrong.

"No", they responded almost in unison and sheepishly as if I caught them doing something wrong.

Then pointing towards the shitter, one of them finally asked, "Hey Chief, what is that guy burning in those barrels behind that little shed?"

I said, "Shit." "They're burning shit."

He quickly turned to the other and said " See I told you so." The second one looked in disbelief and shook his head from side to side.

I guess they had never seen anybody burn shit before. The fifty-five gallon pots were lovingly referred to as "honey pots," no doubt because of their sweet aroma.

Shitters and Pissers In case you hadn't either, here's the lowdown on "honey pots" and shitters. Shitters in Vietnam were very similar to outhouses in Kentucky (or any other rural area in the U.S.). They were made with wooden sides and a corrugated metal roof sloped to the rear. Because of the heat and the need to ventilate the shitters, the top half of the walls were screened. This allowed for ventilation and visibility. Standard toilet seats were placed over the hole or holes and nailed to the plywood seats. (Vietnam shitters came in a variety of sizes—one-holers, two-holers, three holers and even four holers.) Beneath the hole of each toilet seat sits a fifty-five gallon drum that had been cut in half. The drum is filled about 30 % of the way with diesel fuel. Every other day or so, a shit burning detail pulls the pots out from under the shitters and lights them off. The shit burns providing a very distinctive aroma in its black cloud. When the pots burn out they are refueled and put back under the holes.

As one could imagine these shitters were pretty dangerous for careless smokers. Particularly those smokers still having the stateside habit of lifting their asses off the toilet and throwing their lit cigarette in the toilet. Doing this stateside where the toilet is filled with water, there is little danger or cause for concern. In Vietnam where the water has been replaced with diesel fuel the situation is very different. There were a number of legends about guys doing this and being sent home with terrible burns. But I never witnessed it myself. There were also stories of Air Cav troopers using JP4 (jet fuel), instead of diesel and ending up burning up the whole shitter, and sometimes receiving serious burns.

You may not realize it, but shitters were a very important part of our basic living conditions. In fact, every time we moved, we slung load a couple of our shitters with our early lifts to the new area. And yes, there were officers and enlisted shitters.

Of course the squadron didn't have any female shitters, we didn't have any females assigned to us. We had however a French female photographer, Cathy LeRoy, accompany us for a few weeks. We had to make sure she wasn't using the shitter before we went in, since we didn't have a ladies' shitter. I am sure it wouldn't really bother any of us much, but we tried to maintain some sense of civility.

In addition to the shitters we had pissers. I am not too sure of the actual construct of the pissers. Visibly they looked like a tube sticking out of the ground on a 40° angle. In fact they looked like and were about the size of an empty 2.75" rocket tube sticking out of the ground. At Two Bits, a couple of pissers were sticking out the ground on a slope adjacent to our parking revetments. The pissers had white engineer tape attached to the ground in a rectangle about 3 feet wide and 5 feet long. I have no idea why the tape was there. Perhaps the tape was intended to prevent people from inadvertently tripping over or running into it. The first few times I used these pissers I felt pretty weird. There I was standing in the open, aiming down this piss tube, and I could have a conversation with anyone walking back or forth to the flight line, with both of us in full sight of the hooches of the village outside the wire.

There was another design used in pissers as well. These were fifty-five gallon drums with their tops (and to think of it, their bottoms too) cut out and placed in a hole in the ground. At the bottom were some rocks and some chemicals. The top was covered with screening material that was securely fastened to the barrel. Some of these pissers had privacy sides made of canvass. The four corner posts had a three or so foot high canvass stretched from post to post covering three sides. This provided some privacy. Walking by all you could see was from the boot tops down and the waist up, again it didn't interfere with any social conversations.

Today is Sunday! Life in Blue lift had a sameness though. Nothing distinguished one day from another except for Sunday when we were at Duc Pho. Usually we were awoken early in the morning's darkness by Captain Burnham's voice at the entrance to the tent saying: "Rise and shine Blue flight, it's a new day." Don Lewis and McAnally would pump up the Coleman lanterns, as the rest of us would get dressed. Shaving and brushing our teeth was done right outside the tent using makeshift tables made from ammo boxes. We each had our trusty plastic wash basin purchased in downtown An Khe. We would then go to the mess tent for a great Army breakfast. Following breakfast we would head to the Hueys for a preflight. Depending on where we were, we would either go back to the tents as we did in Duc Pho and Two Bits, or mount up and fly out to the forward laager area as we did in Chu Lai. But for the most part everyday began almost the same.

We always knew when Sunday came around. Some chaplain cared enough about it to remind us in a most unique way. Each Sunday morning at Duc Pho a jeep would slowly creep through the LZ with a loudspeaker mounted on its hood. A soft-spoken voice would repeat endlessly the following: " Today is Sunday. . . . Today is Sunday. . . . Catholic services will be held at 9 AM, followed by Protestant services at 9:45. . . . Today is Sunday. . . . Today is Sunday. . . . Today is Sunday. . . . Catholic services . . ."

I don't remember who that Chaplain was who started this, or who the voice was, but thanks to them both, we always knew when a new week started.

Oh! And yes Mom, sometimes I even went up the hill and attended services. Though most days I admit, I did not. Not that I didn't pray! I prayed quite a bit in my time in Vietnam. It's just that I learned you didn't have to be in a church to pray. God heard my prayers wherever I said them. And I am grateful to Him.

As I think about it we also knew when Monday rolled around too. When you went through the chow line for breakfast Top would stand at the head of the chow line and make sure we each swallowed a big orange pill. The pill was an anti-malaria pill, and was supposed to protect us from contracting that disease. All it really did was clog up your intestines for a day or two. On my second tour the Army had improved on their program and in addition to the Big Orange pill on Monday, we had to take a small white pill, about the size of a saccharine pill, on the other days.

New Weapons Research Sometimes we would conduct some very independent research and development on how to better kill the bad guy. Actually, we had a lot of time on our hands between insertions and extractions. Wonder Warthog had come across some mortar rounds. He began dropping a couple out of his aircraft to see how high he needed to go in order to get them to explode. After a few tries, he figured the problem wasn't necessarily the height from which he dropped it, but rather the amount of rotation or spin that armed the rounds. So he went up again and tried to twist the round between the palms of his hands as he released the round. All this did was cause it to bounce off the skids on the way down. He stopped the experiment after realizing that had the round armed it may have exploded on the skids and he may shoot himself down.

Wonder also worked hard as a member of the small bullet betterment team, which was researching how best to make dumb dumb bullets by x-ing, the head of a bullet. Wonder determined the limit of the depth by firing a round that got stuck in the barrel 80% of the way down the barrel. The barrel had a slight bulge towards the tip where the round was lodged.

Tried as he might, he couldn't get the round out. Of course you can't turn in a weapon with a round in the barrel without some good explanation. Even then you would be risking an investigation and some possible fine or punishment. Not that this really mattered to Tom, he devised a plan. He put the gun between two sandbags and carefully aimed it towards the firing berm. With a length of string (light rope) tied around the trigger, and with Tom and Mike and the rest of us crouched down in a low spot in the ground behind the gun, he pulled on the string. Yank! Damn! The gun came tumbling out towards us from between the sand bangs.

He restacked the bags and this time cocked the hammer before we went back to the position. On this second try it fired. Upon inspecting the gun the barrel not only had a bulge but also sported a neat curve to the left. The weapon was in good enough shape for turn in to supply without an explanation.

Others in the troop played with stuffing glass jars with a hand grenade with the pin pulled just before tossing it out of the aircraft. When it hit the hard ground the glass would break, the handle would pop off and a few seconds later the grenade would explode. Or that was the theory. Finding hard ground during the monsoon season was impossible to find. Neither Six, nor the platoon leaders condoned this research at all. But there was a lot going on and they couldn't see everything. We were very lucky that no one got hurt or killed during these activities.

Life in B Troop wasn't restricted to combat flying and otherwise keeping busy between those combat assaults. The troop operated most of the year at forward LZs and not at the base camp in An Khe. For that reason we flew a lot of "ash and trash" missions. Those ash and trash missions were about hauling personnel, equipment, and supplies back and forth from An Khe. We would haul new guys into the field, and old guys out of the field for R&R and to go home. We hauled cases of beer and soda forward to operating LZs.

The slicks always ran the ash and trash missions to An Khe to pick up mail and distribution and FNGs. The mission was usually a good one. First of all, you were probably not gonna get shot at on one of these flights. Second, it's nice to just fly straight and level and enjoy the countryside. And third, as soon as you got to An Khe you could get a ride downtown and get a good steam bath and massage. When you got back everyone was happy to see you because you brought the mail sacks forward. You cannot imagine how important mail from home was.

Care Packages Care packages from home were always a big thing for us. The Army took care of us pretty well we thought. They provided us with "sundry packages." These were boxes of goodies given to supplement the mess hall and try to make up for being away from a PX. The sundry packages would include cartons of cigarettes—Lucky Strike, Pall Mall, Newport, Camels,—candy and chocolate bars, soap and toiletries. Lots of things to munch on and even paperback books to pass the time. But they couldn't compare with care packages from home.

Even stale cookies and soggy cake was welcomed. The folks back home really deserve a standing ovation for meeting our needs (whims??). These were really nice and useful to break up the Army food. From popcorn, to canned anchovies and Ritz crackers, a package from home was heaven. My Mom, brother and sisters made sure that I got at least my fair share of goodies to share with the guys.

Sometimes things didn't work out exactly as planned however. Larry Brown's Mom sent him an ice cream making machine. You know the thing with a crank on it. In any case Larry went to the mess hall this one day and got all the ingredients to make the ice cream. The ice cream mix, the salt, the ice, all the necessary ingredients. About 9:30 or so we began to set this machine up. Under the watchful eyes of the lift pilots, Larry measured the mix, milk, salted the ice and began to crank as we were laagering next to the airstrip at Duc Pho. A few rotations into the cranking the alarm "Launch the Blues" went out. The machine was passed to 35's crew chief, who could be seen through the entire flight, except on short final into the LZ, dutifully cranking away on the handle.

Back to the laager area we continued to crank away and checking the progress. Well it didn't look like the ice cream maker was making much progress. Perhaps the heat and the gook ice prevented it from getting cold enough, soon enough? Who knew? Well after seemingly hours of taking turns cranking it, Larry determined it to be as good as it gets and ceremoniously passed out little cups with ice cream. We took our spoons and together tasted the ice cream. Knowing this was going to be like back home. Well the spoonful was creamy; and it appeared to be vanilla looking and tasting; and was cold; but it wasn't ice cream. The taste was vaguely familiar, however. Finally we identified the taste and the cause. Larry had gotten cake mix from the mess hall. We had been cranking cake mix for the last few hours. I don't know if Larry ever got the recipe right. But I know we will never forget the first time we tried to make ice cream.

Letters Letters and news from home were always welcome. One of my nieces' teachers made me her class project. Miss Watson had the kids draw cards for me and send me letters. They were really cute, and everyone in the section enjoyed looking at some of the things the kids drew and wrote. When I got home I bought ice cream to the class and met Miss Watson. She was a former Miss New York State and really a great looking lady. My brother-in-law and I went on a class picnic with kids once and had a great time with them and Miss Watson. On my second tour (I had received a fixed wing transition and was flying airplanes on a classified mission and was based out of An Khe and Nha Trang.) I found myself staying overnight at a sister company's base in Cam Ranh Bay. That evening we were club hopping among the many clubs at the base. As we passed one area in a club there was a crowd of GIs around this great looking round eye woman. It looked like one of those tours the USO sets up that brought American women ("round eyes") to visit the troops so they would remember what they were fighting for. I walked closer to get a look for myself. Our eyes met and we looked at each other—I said " Miss Watson?" And she said "Uncle John?" And the troops looked at both of us as if we were nuts. We spoke for a short while, then she gave me a miniature New York State flag and we went our separate ways. But can you imagine how small a world it really is?

Letters from Snooks were always welcome and interesting. She was trying to arrange the wedding and coordinate it with me through the Army postal system. It took about a week for mail to get to us. And then it would take another week to get back to her. I don't know how she did it, but the wedding went off like clock-work. There was one effect of me being in Vietnam. Snooks had invited her girlfriend next door to be in her bridal party. A while after accepting the invitation she backed out. Seems her parents were really against the war and had participated in a number of the protests and were giving her a hard time about being in the wedding for one of those guys they were protesting about. Snooks was hurt, but never held it against the girlfriend. In Snooks' letters, she also related all the things that she and my Mom were doing. Snooks would spend almost every weekend with her. They would watch scary movies in bed, each with the covers held under their eyes, ready to hide at the first instance the monster would appear. Her letters also brought news of the family and that was good. I'd read her letters over and over again if the mail was late, or when I was particularly alone.

Writing back became a chore. At first there was a lot of excitement in the stuff we were doing. And I'd write about it. Of course I soon realized that what was fun and exciting for us, was also terrifying for the family back home. Things also changed as the reality set in about what was going on. I stopped writing for a while around November or so. Too busy doing other things, too tired to make conversation. The realities of the days made the problems at home pale. My Mom, or one of my sisters calling on her behalf, contacted the Red Cross, and I had to start writing again. I did okay then and tried to get a letters out every few days.

Writing back home and to Snooks became hard to do. She was planning for a wedding. And me? I didn't know or think I was going to make it home. I knew that for some sinister reason God was keeping me alive only to let me die on my last day in country. I was sort of resigned to it. It didn't play on me or really affect anything I did. I just did what I could and let the rest just happen. But I went along with the wedding plans. I figured if it went the way I suspected, the family could turn the wedding reception into a party for everyone. I had a tough time finding things to write home about without having them worry about me.

Home seemed so far away. In time and distance certainly, but mostly the distance in reality was most noticeable.

I am sure it was as tough for my family back home as it was for me in Vietnam. Snooks not only had me in Vietnam, but also her younger brother Butch. Butch was in the Marines stationed in Da Nang. I tried to visit him once but couldn't find him. Letters from my sisters and their kids were always a highpoint for me. My brother Dave was always my hero; though he says he is my #1 fan. In this mutual admiration undertaking I will tell you Dave is a much better person than me. In the end I realize that I am very fortunate to have a loving and supportive family. I could never thank them too often or too much.

Sometimes we received mail from people we didn't know. Christmas time lots of groups got together and sent cards and letters to the troops. Morale definitely went up when we received these letters, cards, and care packages. I received a letter from a girl who was related to one of the operations radio operators. If I am not mistaken Terry Young had given her my name and address. Terry had been a radio operator with the blues and now was the troop's communications operator. The girl was from Palo Alto California. We exchanged letters for a long while. She was very nice and her letters were always up beat and positive. Right before I left the Troop she sent me a very nice collage and scrapbook which was filled with news of things that happened while I was in Vietnam. It showed the latest fashions and fades in the US, and stuff like that. It described the latest TV shows and top music artists. The scrapbook was such a nice thing to do. She also invited me to stop by and visit on my way back. I didn't stop; maybe I should have stopped to thank her. But I was gonna make it home and I had a girl waiting for me to marry.

Life in Bravo Troop was never dull. We moved around quite a bit. I joined them in Duc Pho. We moved back to An Khe and worked that AO for a couple of weeks. Then we went to Two Bits South. We even went to An Khe for about a week while at Two Bits. Then we went up to Chu Lai and helped with the start of the

Americal Division. The Americal Division was first called Task Force Oregon. We left there and went north to Camp Evans just north of Hue and in time for the offensive of Tet 67. We worked out of there until I left, just as the battle of the Khe San Valley was beginning.

That covers a lot of I Corps, the northernmost war zone in Vietnam.

Pick up Top Jim and I had the honor of transporting our new first sergeant to the field. Jim and I enjoyed clowning around with new guys, and Top (1SG Paul Tyrrell) was to be no exception. We took off from the "Lucky Hot Spot" which was the name for the landing area at the top of the hill where the squadron and troop base camps were. The rear detachment had a small complement of folks who assisted getting us in and out of field for R&R and DEROS.

R&R is the acronym for rest and recuperation. All soldiers were given an R&R during their tour. Most of the R&Rs were out of country for five days or so. Australia was for seven days. The US Forces also ran in-country R&R sites. Vung Tau was probably the most widely used R&R center in Vietnam. It is rumored that both sides sent their troops there for R&R. DEROS is the acronym for Date Estimated Return from Overseas—it is the date that if you survived, you would be returning home. People who rotated home a few days or weeks early were said to have received a "drop."

Lucky Hot Spot was adjacent to the 1/9 Officer's Club the Shenandoah. Shenandoah was a little club, but it could get pretty lively depending on how many of us were back there at a time. The club had an entrance area with hat posts sticking all the way around the area. A big sign was posted above the door that read check your weapons before entering. As we went in, each would remove his weapon and hat and hang them on the hook. On the way out he would pick up his hat and put on his weapon. It reminded me a lot of the old west.

Jim and I had discussed how we would test the new first sergeant and make his first flight with us memorable. We began the flight with an exciting airspeed over altitude takeoff from the Lucky Hot Spot. This maneuver can be described as diving off the top of the hill at low level and maintaining the dive until you pick up the desired airspeed. The maneuver was a little more exciting than a normal takeoff. Jim had told me earlier that one of the parts we had to bring back was a new collective. The collective is one of the primary flight controls used to pilot the aircraft. The collective is located to the left of the pilot and projects through the floor. If the pilot wanted to go up and apply power, he would pull up on the collective. To go down, he would push down on it. Jim had placed the "extra" collective on the floor alongside the real collective on his side of the cockpit.

Jim and I were proceeding at tree top level towards the An Khe pass. On our route two trees stuck up higher than all the rest. We headed straight at them. Jim and I were having a great conversation and looking straight at each other. While unbeknownst to our passengers, we were looking out of the corner of our eyes making sure we didn't hit anything. As the trees got bigger we kept coming. At the last moment before we were to "hit" the trees we both turned forward and yelled while Jim pulled up on the dummy collective exposing the end of it with all the loose wires hanging out of it. I pulled up on the real collective ensuring we were going to miss the trees. We had a good laugh at ol'Top that day.

Top Top, First Sergeant Paul Tyrell wasn't really excited to be coming to the Air CAV. He was a tanker by MOS and training. In the Air CAV he had all of these officers and pilots, and a platoon of grunts to deal with. Top was a soldier though and the troops, all of us, grew to love the guy. Top was an old man to us though in reality he was only 29 years old. But Top was a great soldier.

One late afternoon at Two Bits we were sent out on a special single ship mission. We were to take a squad of the Blues and go to meet up with either a Green Beret or a LRRP Team in the mountains south-southwest of Two Bits. We were to bring back a couple of prisoners they had captured. We were given their radio frequency and told to be careful and try not to give their position away too soon. Top decided to go out with the squad on this mission. He would go out with each squad, showing the young troops that he was not afraid to do what they do, and that he would do his part. He taught us all about leadership without saying one word. All you needed to do was watch. That's the way we learned about leadership in B Troop, and I suspect the entire Squadron. You learned the important lessons of the profession by watching and doing. What a leadership academy!

We came upon the area that was the mouth of about three different valleys. There were many mountaintops and ridgelines, and the LRRP or Special Forces guys could be anywhere. Of course so could the bad guys; this was indian country to be sure. We contacted them and they said they were going to pop green smoke. Immediately we saw green smoke in two different areas. Someone was playing games. We told them to pop smoke and we would identify the color. I had also tuned in the FM homing to get a line bearing on the radio they were using. They rogered the transmission and said smoke was out. Again two smokes went out. This time they were different colors. We identified yellow smoke and they confirmed. Our FM Homing confirmed the direction, and we quickly headed to the LZ.

We began the approach to the hilltop the area was unimproved and grown up pretty bad. There was no room to set down on the ground. What we did was hover in and plant the front of the skids on the ground and hold the bird teetering there with the rear of the skids and tail of the Huey extending out over the top side of the hill slopping rapidly away. There was probably a 20 foot drop from the aft of skids to the ground. The Blues and Top, got on the skids and walked forward until they were on the ground. We would more likely crash than get shot down, though both eventualities were possible. They got the prisoners and brought them back the same way. Hovering there took our full attention, never mind worrying about who the other smoke throwers were. When Top and the Blues were aboard we took off backwards, peddle turned and got out of there. We avoided the area where that second smoke came up.

We dropped the prisoners off at the PW compound, went to refuel and came back to Two Bits.

Top really impressed me. He was a neat guy and good soldier. I kind of felt sorry for him having all of these officer pilots in his unit and only a small group of enlisted men and NCOs to do all of the work. But Top did well.

Top and his lovely lady came to a couple of VHPA reunions. It is always great seeing him and being in his company. I think we appreciate him more today than we did then because we didn't know all the things he was doing for us.

The Famous Picture—Bravo Blues

One of the most used and most famous pictures that came from the Vietnam War is one showing a Huey at a hover with infantrymen jumping down out of it. A U.S Army photographer took the photo. In the foreground can be seen other infantrymen and a radio operator. I have a picture of the photograph on my wall . Over the years when I would be out and about I would often come across the photo, either in a magazine, or on a calendar, or on someone's wall, I would stop and look at it.

I have heard many a story over these years from people who knew someone who's commander, or friend had been assigned to some unit, and that this guy was one of the pilots flying that aircraft that day. It is always so interesting. When I or any of the lift pilots or our Blues, look at that aircraft we see the distinctive yellow square on the pilots door, just like we had on ours signifying that we were in B Troop. A Troop had a yellow triangle, and C Troop a yellow circle. A = angle, B = box, C = circle. Most of the CAV adopted this convention in marking their aircraft, and it may have been countrywide. Some units added to the basic symbol with a lightning bolt, or a flying horseshoe, or something like that. When we got our new H models we added the aircraft commander's call sign inside the box. Thus in the center of my yellow square were the numerals 3 and 7 for Saber Blue 37.

Returning to the picture, we notice the infantryman in the foreground looking back towards the helicopter and recognize him as being LT Ted Chilcote, our Blue platoon leader. Jumping out of the aircraft we see the platoon sergeant SFC Richard Wilkerson. There is some discussion about who is next on the skid. Many believe it is Bob Lackey, but we have not been able to conclusively identify who it is. There is no doubt about the next man. He is Jimmy Cryster and the RTO who got killed up at Chu Lai. He was shot in the neck on the insertion that started the battle on 13 November 1967. Jimmy never left the aircraft; they flew him immediately back to Chu Lai. The next day on 14 November I went to the hospital to visit him. He was laying in bed with machines hooked to him. He was clean, appeared to be in no pain, but also he appeared very, very bad. The Blues went over to visit when they got back on the 14th as well. That evening Jimmy died. His family hadn't heard the either the full story or the true story until mid year 2000. Some pretender had contacted the family and told the mother that Jimmy died alone in a rice paddy. He went on to say that all the other guys in the photo were dead. Nothing he said was correct. A group of us became aware of this through the Bullwhip Association. Each of us who knew what happened wrote letters (or e-mailed) to Jimmy's family telling them what really happened. They responded and were very pleased and comforted to know he was not alone when he died. And that he had been visited by us and that we had not forgotten about him, either that day in Vietnam, or 33 years later. We had a Bullwhip Reunion at Fort Rucker in the fall of 2000 and Jimmy's sister and her two daughters came down and met with us. I think we all felt good about setting the record straight and helping these wonderful folks who have suffered so long. The picture was taken west-southwest of Duc Pho. The LZ was a one ship LZ to a pinnacle or hilltop LZ. From the famous picture it is difficult to tell who among the Blue pilots was flying. We know it couldn't be 35, because 35 was always the lead and there are troops on the ground. Blue used to fly in on the second ship so that would eliminate 36, McAnally. That leaves only Don Lewis (38) or Jim Pratt (39). From a couple of other photos which were taken by the photographer at the same time there is one that makes it appear that on the rear of the helmet on the pilot in the right seat there is something square on it.

Jim Pratt had a photo of a naked girl kneeling on a chair scotch taped to the back of his helmet. Don Lewis didn't have anything on his helmet. He certainly wouldn't have a naked woman on there. That's for sure. (Don was the old guy in the platoon. He had spent a lot of years in the Air Force and transferred for flight school. He went through flight school as a warrant officer because of his age and the fact that he was already a commercial fixed wing pilot.)

So the aircraft commander in that photo is probably Jim Pratt. Who is flying with him? We don't really know. The most likely contenders are Mike Covey, Wonder Warthog, or me. Each has a number of supporters who will swear that it had to be so and so. I don't think anyone really cares who flew the bird in the picture that day. We all flew in there on that flight on that day. And we are proud to have been in the unit that for some epitomized the Huey in Vietnam.

What further complicates the issue is that the photographer took pictures of many of our insertions that day in the mountains. And many of them were very similar. In one set that Pratt had gotten from the National Archives shows an almost identical picture but the Blues are riding on a different aircraft. So who really knows who was flying in that picture?

The place could go to the dogs quickly Jim and I were flying combat assaults out of Duc Pho this one day. The flight had put the Blues in on the west side of a village which was bordered on the east by the beach.

Working the beaches was a real bummer. The Hueys rotor wash is pretty powerful. Landing or taking off from the beach causes the sand to be drawn up and down through the blades and of course into the aircraft through the open doors and widows. Of course it would settle into everything. I can still feel the rawness of my back on those days after working in the beach areas. The sand down the back and then rubbed into the skin as the Huey bounced and vibrated for the rest of the day.

They swept the village and called for pickup. The landing was no problem at all. Just the usual routine, we shot the approach to the ground to minimize the blowing sand. The LZ was cold and there was no real rush. The Blues climbed aboard and the crew chief said we were up. Usually when the Blues were all on board in cold PZs like this, we would call the lead (35) and tell him the flight was up. This is one of the jobs of the trail aircraft in cold LZs and PZs. This to make sure we didn't leave anyone in the PZ. As I reached down for the radio on the center console to switch my communications selector from Intercom to UHF radio (the air communications channel) I was shocked. Here was this enormous head with a gigantic slobbering tongue hanging from between big canine teeth inches away from my face. When did the goddamn dog get on! The dog was leaning with his front paws on the radio console looking out the front windscreen. The radio console, where his big front paws were, was like a pedestal with the top of the console about 18" high, and separated the pilot and co-pilot. He was panting and slobbering on the console.

Using the floor mike switch, I keyed the intercom with my

right foot to get Jim's attention and said to Jim over the intercom "Hey Jim I'll fly the bird out, you call 35."

Jim looked over towards me as he went to take his hands off the controls and the shock on his face was priceless. We played this "you do it; no you do it" game for a few seconds until 35 called and asked "Three-nine we up yet?"

I gently reached down, amid the slobber, quickly switched the selector and said "Roger three-five your er . . . er..er..upfff!" Jim cracked up laughing and I flew the bird out of the LZ. No one knew what we were laughing at until we got back home and we retold the story to the other crews and the Blues.

U.S. Army Photo
Bravo Blue squad leader Barry Mc Alpine and another
Blue (Pancho) in the background were pictured with
the tracker dog and the dog handler.

My biggest problem was the sand getting down my back where it would just grind up and down in beat with the whop-whop-whop of the blades. Many a day my back felt raw from the sand and sweat.

The dog was part of a tracker team that was assigned to the Blues for a few weeks while we were in Duc Pho. Typically the dogs would just curl up under the handler's seat and jump out with the handler. On one assault we had to go into a single ship LZ in the mountains. The LZ was real small and required us to sort of hover down beneath the tops of the surrounding trees. We came in and as the Blues jumped off from about five feet and we began a slow takeoff climb back up through the opening in the trees. All of a sudden the crew chief started yelling I looked back and down and saw the handler and Blues yelling and pointing.

"The dog!" Dunn yelled. "The damn dog didn't jump!"

The dog was still under the damn seat. We aborted the climb at about 30 feet in the air and backed down the takeoff angle until we were at a low hover. Now this is not a good place to be for a helicopter—sitting in an LZ for all the bad guys to take a bead on. Nor was it a good maneuver to back down a take off angle into a rough LZ either. Thankfully the handler was able to coax the dog out from under the seat and we were able to get the hell out of there. We sort of got on the crew chief because he wouldn't stick his hand under the seat and drag the dog out. We had a good laugh over that one too.

Dogs weren't the only animals we carried aboard our aircraft. A ville just north of Duc Pho was being pacified, or some other similar program. The way this worked was we would drop the Blues into the ville and they would herd all the villagers with a limited amount of their must-have possessions out to one side of the ville. Then we would come in and start hauling them to a new settlement that had been built by the South Vietnamese government. The new place would have wood walls and metal roofs. Very similar to what many of the rear echelon troops lived in.

The mission was really wild. We would herd lots of little people on each of the slicks. There they would it on the floor and grab and hold onto anything that appeared to be attached to the aircraft. For many of these folks this was the first time they were in anything that had an engine, let alone a helicopter! I remember on one lift a small boy, just tall enough to peer over my seat, clutched to the back of my seat. I turned and watched his eyes get bigger and bigger as we took off and flew to the new settlement. The young guy seemed to be enjoying his first flight. He smiled the whole time.

Other passengers weren't so happy. They climbed all over themselves and their fellow villagers to get away from the wide openings of the doors. Of course we didn't close the doors because of the heat. The open doors helped to cool it off some. And besides these villagers didn't smell very good at all. Not only their bad breath but the body odor was terrible. A couple of the villagers carried aboard chickens and at least one tried to bring a pig along. Neither he, nor his pig got on my aircraft. I left him on the ground. The aircraft smelled pretty bad for the next couple of days.

The village was burned to the ground after the villagers were evacuated in order to deny the VC the use of it. I suspect it also ensured the villagers couldn't move back once they saw their new compounds.

White Mice We also carried some South Vietnamese units including the National Police. "White Mice" they were dubbed because of their white cab driver hats. The white mice would go in with the ARVN (Army of Vietnam) soldiers to the various villages and interrogate the villagers. I suspect some of them were Viet Cong at night, but what do I know?

When we carried the ARVN and White Mice the crewchief's duties became a little more intense. When we would go in to pick them up, he made sure to keep his weapon at the ready in case one of them decided to switch sides and become a hero by taking a Huey out of action. Similarly, in the LZ he made sure that when they got out they didn't leave any goodies behind to include hand grenades and satchel charges.

I never felt quite safe having these guys in the back seat with all of those weapons. They not only took their weapons with them they took their own food. Unlike our Blues and other US troops who carried C-rations with them, the ARVNs carried chickens and small pigs for rations. What a way to wage war, went through my mind more than once while carrying these guys.

The Flight From Hell Right about the time I was to make Aircraft Commander and given my own callsign—instead of being Jim's or another aircraft commander's X-ray—we began receiving the new H model Huey. The H model looked almost exactly the same as the D model. However the pitot tube (the primary air intake that is used for the airspeed indicator) was moved to the top of the aircraft from its original location just below the windshield. And the 2 FM homing antenna on the nose of the aircraft were removed. These were the only real changes you could see from the outside. The big changes in the H model were in the engine.

The D models we had were equipped with L11 engines while the H models had L13s. The L11s developed 1100 shaft horsepower while the L13 developed 1400 horsepower. When we first received the H models we were told we could pull more than the 50 pounds of torque we were limited to in the D Models. Torque was the measurement used to gauge the amount of demand or power you were putting on the turbine engine. It is used as the manifold pressure readings are used in reciprocating engines of the older helicopters, and non-turbine aircraft. I think they initially said we could pull 52 or 54 pounds. Since in the D models, due to the high temperatures we could only pull about 45 pounds of torque before you began to bleed off RPM, I don't think we ever pulled in more than about 48 pounds of torque. Those new aircraft were beautiful. They would leap into the air compared to the older D models. Pretty soon though they changed the limitation back to the old D model limit of 50 pounds. I think the deal was the engine could take the higher torque but the transmission or the tail rotor drive system couldn't. In any case we were soon operating back in the old limits. But that was okay, we still had a stronger aircraft.

As would be expected, rank has its privileges, the first H model to come in was given to the platoon leader, Blue 35. And then the new H models were issued to the pilots in numerical order. 35, 36, etc. For a while there, old Jim and I were being left in the dust. Everyone else in front of us in the formation had these nice, new, strong aircraft. Jim and I were stuck in the back of the formation struggling with the old dog model battling the dirty air. Shortly before our turn in came I became an aircraft commander and got my own aircraft and call sign. I was now, Saber Blue 37.

Saber Blue 37 with his new H Model Huey—"Baby Snooks"—named for his girlfriend. Photo courtesy of Loren Mc Anally

The B Troop Blue Lift Flight now consisted of Saber Blue Three-five Captain Don Burnham, Blue Three-six, Loren McAnally, Blue Three-seven John Flanagan, Blue Three-nine Jim Pratt. We flew that line up for a longtime. Eventually, Mike Covey became Blue 38, and Captain Nubbs Hirning took over for CPT Burnham, and Wonder Warthog took over for McAnally.

In any case it came time to pick up some more new aircraft in Saigon. In order to do that we had to turn in the old ones. The turn-in and issue operation was under the control of some major at squadron. I think he was the squadron maintenance officer. He was an old fixed wing guy and not the most personable guy in the world. In fact I don't remember any pleasant conversations or interchanges with him at all. Before we left the Troop area our maintenance section pulled out all the good equipment, replacing it with inoperable stuff. By this I mean, all the instruments and the best radios and equipment were stripped off the aircraft. In their place were installed inoperative gauges and barely functioning equipment. In addition to this, we had one of the fuel boost pumps inoperative, putting the aircraft in a circled red "X" condition.

The Army uses a code to indicate the maintenance condition of each piece of equipment. The codes run from a "Dash" indicating the aircraft is in great shape, through a diagonal which indicates a minor system deficiency or a routine inspection was due, to the Red X which indicates the aircraft is not flyable. Now for some Red X conditions, that affect or restrict only certain kinds of flights the red X is circled. This allowed you to fly the aircraft in any of its unrestricted or unaffected modes of operation. For example, if you didn't have an operating attitude indicator, which is used in instrument flight, you could still fly the aircraft VFR. (Visual Flight Rules), but were not permitted to fly in instrument conditions.

Having only one electric boost pump restricted the aircraft to flights below 10,000 feet. This, because the engine driven pump could not operate efficiently enough on its own above the 10,000 foot pressure altitude without the boosted pressure from the boost pump. Now you have two electric boost pumps one on each side, but if one was out already and you were above 10000 feet and the second boost pump went out you might lose the entire engine due to fuel exhaustion.

Because of the normal daily condition of the aircraft—old and beat up—compounded by the maintenance team's activities, the aircraft Jim and I had was filled with diagonals and circled Red Xs. We were restricted to VFR flight, and flight below 10,000. After much preparation and activity we finally got all of the paperwork together and put the other required equipment on board and were ready to turn in the aircraft. The flight took off enroute to Saigon with a refueling stop planned at Nha Trang. There were three birds in the flight. The major took the lead followed by Mike Covey and McAnally, and then Jim and I pulling up the rear as usual.

I'll bet we were up at 5000 feet. Now that isn't really that high except when you consider we flew mostly at tree top level. If not at tree top level, we would be at 1000 feet. Above 1000 feet was almost nosebleed altitude for us. As the flight progressed, Jim and I and Earl Hobbs our crewchief just bullshitted away as we normally did. After a while we began to notice that a layer of clouds was forming below us. We talked about this and then on the platoon frequency to Mc Anally and Wonder. Finally we called the Major and voiced our concerns. You see we are up there and our instrument flight instruments were not working.

The Major said "no sweat we'll find a hole to let down through or we can shoot an instrument approach in formation." Yeah right. We're gonna take the flight into the clouds and fly formation? There was a lot of chatter on the radio over this between us B Troop pilots as we discussed this guy's parentage and his insanity. The major couldn't hear us, we were on our own frequency. I was to learn later that you can fly a tight formation in the clouds but it is not something we were going to do with so little actual instrument experience.

As the flight progressed we went higher and higher to get over the clouds which were building in front of us. Things did not look good for us. We were at 10000 feet for a short while during that leg. With only one fuel boost pump we were at risk of losing the engine had the remaining pump gone out, because the engine driven pump couldn't maintain pressure about 10000 feet. Jim and I had already learned the importance of fuels pumps the month before when we lost the engine and had to autorotate for real into a rice paddy.

Now I wasn't an instrument pilot, neither was Jim, and besides, this aircraft had no operating instruments, so we were doomed to the formation instrument option unless we could find a hole. The other guys were not any happier than we were about our predicament.

Arriving over Nha Trang we learned the weather was VFR with a 1000 foot ceiling (i.e. the base of the clouds were about that 1000 feet above the ground). We began to look around for a hole as we started our descent down from our lofty altitude. Luckily we found a hole just to the north of the airfield and did a joined needle autorotation. A joined needle autorotation is when you keep the engine running but you descend as if wasn't. This provided the fastest rate of descent, and we needed to get down before the hole closed up. Here went the entire flight, falling from the sky in a tight spiral. We descended through a couple of thousand feet of sucker hole in the clouds. Though a dizzying flight path, it had to be better than trying to fly formation in the clouds with no instruments.

We finally got down, refueled and shut down. During our post flight inspection Earl Hobbs our crew chief for this mission noticed something loose on the head. He went over to some other crew chiefs that were assigned at Nha Trang in one of those VIP flight detachments I was supposed to go to. There they were working on their spotless highly polished aircraft while we were in a dirty mismatched painted Huey with the yellow crossed sabers on the nose and the yellow squares on the doors, which had seen her better days. We were definitely from the other side of the tracks here. Earl asked to borrow some wrenches and some safety wire. They obliged him and watched as Earl climbed atop the Huey and began tightening the bolts and "torquing" them down. Earl finished what he was doing, returned the tools and we went to lunch. As we walked away together, the other crewchiefs just watched and shook their heads in disbelief.

Lunch gave us some time to talk to one another and make some decisions on our own. Because the weather was dropping, we were able to convince the Major that we weren't going to go VFR on top anymore that day. And that we had decided to go out below the clouds. That is, we were going to fly low level the rest of the way to Saigon. Who knows how many bad guys we are going to overfly enroute to the destination, and us with no gun cover? No gun cover? Why worry about that, we didn't even have any maps of where we were going. We did have a useless "one over the world" scale maps similar to an Eastern United States road map for which the Automobile Association of America (AAA) is so famous. Who cared about the small stuff, this had to be better than falling out of a cloud and going in upside down. We were used to low level, and if we were going in we were going in under control and on our own terms.

The weather got worse the farther we went. The worse it got the lower we went, and the lower the visibility got. The lower the visibility, the closer we got to each other and the more lights we put on. With no instruments and no maps for the area it had the makings of a really big disaster. We flew and we flew, and we had no idea where in the hell we were. This major was a catastrophe looking for a place to happen! And we were going to go with him.

We were getting pretty low on fuel and that was adding to the uneasiness of the flight. We came flying across some compound at about 40 feet that the Major thought was where we wanted to be. Unfortunately we found out we weren't where he thought we were. Fortunately there was a refueling point there and we topped off the tanks again. We were lucky to find the fuel, before we got more than five minutes into the 20-minute fuel warning light. This 20-minute light didn't work as well as one would think.

Gassed up we hovered out again. We were actually not flying; we were at a high fast hover as we followed the major looking for the right LZ. We were listening to the major talking to the control towers during all this stuff. It soon became obvious he didn't know where we were, and the tower didn't have any idea either. This guy was certifiably dangerous. Finally, he found the area he was looking for and we all pulled into the area for parking.

The parking area had revetments there. The only one left when Jim and I pulled in had a big sign proclaiming that this spot was reserved for the maintenance officer. I parked there. I was pissed and tired, and didn't give a damn about some maintenance officer's parking spot. I was trying to keep myself from wanting to kill the damn major. Some mechanic or technical inspector from the unit came over to us all excited and told me I had to move the aircraft because the spot was reserved for the maintenance officer. Like I didn't know how to read. I told him in no uncertain terms that I'd move it after the turn-in inspection and not before.

We all went inside the maintenance hut and after hitting the head began exchanging the paperwork to turn the Hueys in and draw the new ones. While we did this, the mechanics were inspecting and inventorying our aircraft. They had to make sure we were turning in all the stuff that came with the aircraft. Of course it didn't matter that it didn't work, just so long as all of the equipment was there, and the logbooks reflected they were inoperative. During this process they also ensured the aircraft were in a flyable condition.

I don't know how long the inspection took, perhaps 45 minutes or an hour. Finally the guys who were inspecting my bird came in. I asked if they were finished and they said, "Yes." I called to Earl and said "let's go," and asked the mechanics where they wanted me to move the aircraft. They looked at Earl and me as if we were crazy. I asked again. This time one of them replied, "Mister, I wouldn't pick that aircraft to a hover. We found 17 Red X's on it!"

We had just come from way up north from flying from 10000 feet to 20 feet, over 3/4s of the NVA and VC army and now they tell us the birds are unsafe to hover another hundred yards or so to the turn in pads? Oh well. I just love being in the CAV.

We pre-flighted the new birds and got out of there as fast as we could and headed to Vung Tau for the night. Vung Tau was on the coast, and was an in country R&R (rest and recuperation) center. There were rumors that the NVA and VC used it for R&R as well as the US and allied forces. It certainly was a beautiful place with a beautiful beach and near stateside accommodations.

We stayed at the Pacific Hotel. Jim and I shared a room, as did Mac and Covey. The major and the captain got individual rooms I think. Or maybe the captain was smart enough to stay alone rather than risk catching some of the major's insanity. The hotel was okay, and much better than the tent we were living in up north. And it had real beds, clean sheets, running water, a shower, and a flush toilet! Man, this was living.

When we got into our room, Jim noticed there was a little lizard crawling on one of the walls. He went to the desk to complain. He returned saying the clerk apologized. He went on to say the clerk was very sorry because we were supposed to have two lizards per room. That's the way they controlled the insects and bugs in their hotel. The lizards were low-tech bug zappers. I don't know what they did at night, I just told myself they stayed on the wall, and wouldn't dare come into the bed or approach a human. Though I am sure they did close recons of us during the night.

Our night in Vung Tau was a kicker from the start. You've got to remember we had just put in a very, very long and hairy day of flying. The entire flight was intense. And the time to relax had come. And boy were we ready to relax. First off we had brought civilian clothes with us from our clothes we had stored in An Khe, but we all needed civilian shoes. We landed just a short distance from a PX annex and just a short time before it closed. We sent Mike Covey (I think) out to buy shoes for us before the PX closed. He came back and handed the shoeboxes out to us as we secured the aircraft for the night. Well as luck would have it, when we get to the hotel and I tried on my shoes I found I had two right loafers! No, no one had two left loafers; I just had two right loafers. So I spent the night in Vung Tau with 2 right shoes. My predicament served as the source of great joy for the others joy and fuel for much harassment directed at me. They were quick to point out to all the young maidens and others my ill-fitting shoes. That's the least I could do for them, I thought,—bring joy and laughter to my comrades.

A group of Australians were staying at the hotel at the same time. These guys were absolutely wild, and were the favorites of the young ladies who frequented the night. Each of the Aussies had at least two girls on their arms and they were deep into par-tying hardy. We went out and toured the city in the pedicabs. (Pratt will probably tell you we were looking for the Art Museum, but we weren't. We were just out having fun.) Pedicabs are those tricycles with the two seats in front and the guy pedals from the back. We had a great time. We drank and drank, and went to the next place, and drank some more. We laughed and laughed and made absolute fools of ourselves, I am sure.

I think Pratt started a race between the cabdrivers promising large amounts of money if his cab beat the others. We went crazy that night-not bad crazy, good crazy. We got to bed at some time that night. We woke up sometime the next morning as planned and went to the flight line for the trip back. The head hurt a bit in the morning, and we were not looking forward to another flight as we had the day before. Luckily for us the weather had improved and the day looked bright.

Returning to the Troop was essentially uneventful. The weather was a lot better. I flew with the captain. I was the only one who was still current in the Charlie model so I flew the Charlie model back, and got the captain current in it on the way. The C model was a good flying gunbird though they had a characteris-tic a bounce to it caused by its 540 main rotor system. The Charlie model was especially nice when unloaded and as new as this one was.

I returned to Vung Tau sometime later in my tour on a three day, in-country R&R. I don't remember anything much except drinking "33" beer on the beach surrounded by a mix of military aged US and Vietnamese males. The music was pretty loud too. I stayed in a villa that one of the southern corps helicopter units had across from the R&R center. I had run into one of the pilots from this unit in the R&R center and we struck up a conversation. Since I hadn't any reservations he invited me to stay at the villa. The villa was nice and clean and cheap. I remember the bed. A good size double bed with four long bedposts that held up a pure white mosquito net awaited me. Once inside the netting, I felt surrounded by a white lace world. What a comfortable and peaceful feeling I had while in there. I guess I was safe in that house. I didn't much think of danger when away from the unit and on R&R.

We were very fortunate that the major didn't get us killed on that flight to Saigon and back. Later in the tour he was leading a flight of brand new WO1 pilots with new OH6 scout aircraft from An Khe to Camp Evans. Again the weather was bad. As they came through the An Khe pass, the major took the flight IFR (into the clouds) to get on top of the clouds. A couple of the aircraft ended up crashing into the mountain killing the crews and destroying the aircraft. What a waste!

I heard that the major was killed some years later in an aircraft accident involving flying IFR in South or Central America

The Takeoff Light The H model Huey was different from the D models. The engines were bigger, the instruments worked, it looked good and it smelled new.

After flying the H models for a week out in the AO you really loved all that extra power. The D model was so under powered that during most takeoffs you had to bleed off RPMs and almost make a running or bouncing takeoff. If you pulled the collective up too high i.e. demand more power that the aircraft had, the result would be a decrease in your rotor rpm. The engine was just not strong enough to pull the loads we were carrying. When that happened a big red RPM light illuminated on the console. It indicated that your RPM was reaching its limit. If you continued and pulled more rpm off a hi-pitched warning tone would sound in your helmet as the light continued to shine. The combination of the big red light and the loud whooop-whooop-whooop audio going off in your ears would definitely get your attention.

One night, a couple of weeks after us all getting the H models, we were sitting around outside the tents shooting the bull with each other and some of the Blues. We spent most nights like that. Just sitting out at the end of tents in the moonlight aided by the Coleman lantern. We would just sit in our folding beach chairs and shoot the shit. This was the equivalent of going out on the deck or patio in the real world and relaxing before bed. The evenings were always a time to enjoy good conversation and share some laughs. This night the conversation turned to the subject of helicopters, as it tended to when the Blues joined in.

This night I asked one of the Blues how he liked the new aircraft. I was surprised when he shook his head back and forth and said he didn't like it at all. "Especially coming out of the LZ" he said.

I was really surprised. This was the first criticism I had heard of the new more powerful H Model. This was really strange, with the D model we were really struggling to get out of the LZs with the Blues we were carrying. Especially when flying with Jim Pratt in the last aircraft in the formation. We not only had a load, we had dirty air from the others rotor blades to contend with. But now, with the H Model, we could come out of the LZ without pulling off any rpm at all.

I pressed him and asked what his reasons were for not liking the H models. I said, "What's wrong with the H Model?"

He said " The Takeoff light doesn't work."

"The takeoff light?" I said.

"What take off light" I asked incredulously. "There is no such thing as a takeoff light."

He said, "You know, Mister F. In the old Hueys when we got

ready to take off from the LZ, you would pick us up to that low hover right? Then you would move forward real slow, right?"

I nodded again. He went on,

"And then right before we took off that red light would come on telling us everything was ready and okay to go. Then the helicopter would shake and shudder and we were flying. Now we don't see the light. I don't like the H model!"

I almost wet my pants laughing and rolling on the ground. The other pilots and the crew chiefs were rolling with laughter as well as the poor blue looked at us as if we were crazy. What he thought was a "take off light" was really the low rpm warning light, indicating we were losing rpm and running out of power. When I told him what was really happening, he seemed a little embarrassed, but satisfied for a while.

Then he looked worried again and said "You mean all those times that light was on we were in trouble?"

I said "Yep!"

He went back to his tent shaking his head.

Chapter Ten

An Khe—Dave Bressam

The troop was called back to An Khe for a couple of weeks to work out around the base camp and provide additional security for the division's base camp. These were some fun days. The squadron area was located on a hill adjacent to the Golf Course. The Golf Course was the large level field where the 1st Air Cavalry Division had cleared to accommodate all of their helicopters. The area was huge and filled row upon row with revetments to protect the aircraft from rocket and mortar fire.

A small road led from the golf course to the top of the hill. Metal roofed, wood and screen sided buildings were scattered along both sides of the road. The buildings belonged to each of the troops and the squadron headquarters. This was the rear area for the 1/9 Cavalry. It served as the processing and administrative center for the troops. Behind the Squadron was a corral that once housed the mule that Colonel J.B. Stockton—Bull Whip 6—brought over to Vietnam as the 1/9 's mascot.

Towards the top of the hill were a few more buildings that were partitioned into two man rooms that served as the B Troop officer's hooches. At the very top of the hill was the 1/9 Cavalry's officer's club the Shenandoah. Close by was a small helipad, big enough for perhaps three of four Hueys—we called it the Lucky Hot Spot.

The rear detachments took care of picking up the FNGs and getting the short timers out on time. Our rear detachment commander was typically the former Blue platoon leader. Most times Blue would only stay in the field for 6 months then he would be sent to the rear. He had paid his dues.

One day we were going to put the Blues on the ground to sweep an area on the other side of Hong Kong Mountain. Dave Bressam also a classmate of mine was flying guns at the time. Dave had the day off and decided to go on the ground with the Blues. It had been done before and many of us had planned to do it also.

Our typical assault to an area was a work of art. Our FO (artillery forward observer) would go out in the area in a scout aircraft and shoot some artillery registration rounds. He would adjust the guns until they hit the coordinates he wanted. When he was set and at the pre-determined time he would shift the fires to the intended LZ. He would prep the LZ for about 20 minutes. Pounding the LZ with artillery rounds made sure there wasn't anything lying in there that would get us when we came in. It also served to keep the bad guys heads down as well.

As the prep was going on, the assault force would form up. Typically Saber 6 would be in his gun ship in the lead flying down our final approach course. Behind and above him we would have a team from Blue Max the ARA (Aerial Rocket Artillery). Blue Max had Huey hogs. These Hueys carried 48 rockets per bird and were able to fire them in pairs, multiple pairs or a salvo where all the rockets fired at the same time.

Behind and below Blue Max we would come—Blue Lift—in a tight diamond formation. Alongside of us we would have one of our gunships. The scouts would be off to the sides ready to work over the Blues once we got them on the ground.

The FO would arrange that the last round fired from the artillery wound be a Willy Peter (WP = white phosphorus). This was readily identifiable because of its white brilliant smoke and burning embers. Once the last round was in the LZ 6 would lead the gaggle down the approach course and mark the specific LZ with his rockets and then break off. This would free Blue Max to continue the prep with their loads. As we got to the point on the approach where we had to begin to slow down for the landing, our guns would maintain speed and begin the final covering fires while we shot the landing. 6 and his wingman would have begun setting up the pattern to protect the guns and us on the takeoff. We would come into the LZ and at from 3—5 feet, though sometimes higher—much higher—the Blues would jump off the skids and move quickly away from the aircraft and seek cover positions, providing covering fire as we departed the LZ.

We had done these so many times that it became a well-scripted movement. From the time the artillery fire was lifted until we were out was no more than 2 or 3 minutes. Last round, 6 marks, Blue Max fires, short final, Red Birds pass us firing on the tree lines, "we're up," Blue flight on the go from the LZ, breaking right in the climb, we're clear. Piece of cake. What a beautiful scene to watch! The precision, the teamwork, everyone doing their job the best they could. Professionals every one of them was a professional.

This day however, would be different. Damn it!

The artillery prep went according to plans. Because of the size of the LZ we were spaced out in a trail formation. The formation was Blue 35, 36, 37 (me), and 39. We spaced ourselves out so that as the first ship was departing the LZ, the next one was landing. Saber 6 fired his rockets and began his break. I watched as Blue Max started their run with the traditional lowering of the nose to begin the dive and commence firing. Then it happened. For some unknown reason the Blue Max on the right side almost came to a stop and began to pivot to the right. I could see his tail rotor slowly windmilling. His nose was going down turning right, he was coming through about 200 degrees of turn he was facing us now. He was in trouble, big trouble. He was punching off rockets all the way. Fired a few pairs in our direction. We continued on the approach. Obviously he had lost his tail rotor. In those days, we were taught to cut the power to the engine and attempt an autorotation to the ground.

The crew did just that. I saw them go in almost vertically into the trees. They went in relatively level. They went down into the trees and appeared to bounce back up a little and then disappeared out of sight.

35 was on short final into the LZ. 36 called that he was breaking out and following the downed bird. I continued the approach to the LZ, as did 39. Our guns and scouts split up with some providing cover over the LZ and while the others stayed over the downed bird.

36 arrived over the site but there was no place to set down. He found a place where the trees were the shortest. The headquarters squad, with Dave Bressam, jumped down through the trees. The trees were about fifteen or twenty feet high.

36, 39 and I had inserted our Blues and took off from the original LZ as planned. We climbed up in formation. Monitoring the radios for information on both of the sites where we had put the Blues in and at the crash site.

The headquarters squad moved quickly to the wreckage. As they came upon the aircraft and started to pull the crew out, the ship exploded.

We saw the explosion. My stomach dropped. Then the radio chatter began telling the story of the tragedy. Our Blues had just gotten to the ARA ship when the fuel tank exploded sending our Blues in all directions.

We went in and extracted the Blues and put them into a clearing a ways from the crash site. The Blues humped the distance quickly to their comrades. Medevac, who had been called as soon as Blue Max went in, was on scene almost immediately. They used the winch to haul up our wounded and dying. We passed over the site and lowered our on-board fire extinguishers. Not that they would do much now, but this was the only thing we could do at the time.

Dave. Doc. And others, whose names escape me right now,

were hurt pretty bad, and a couple of our guys were KIA from the explosion. As I recall, two aboard the ARA ship survived, but they too, were badly wounded.

I made lots of trips back and forth to the site. The flights are mostly a blur. I recall carrying out and lowering chain saws to the Blues. The Blues hacked out the area so make air re-supply easier and safer. One flight that I do recall, however. The Blues had opened the crash site area a bit by knocking down some trees, so that there was hole just big enough for a Huey to hover down. I was the first to use it. More correctly, I was the first to try to hover down the hole. I shot the approach to terminate at a high hover right on the top of the hole. This is not the smartest, safest or most tactically correct thing to do. The only way to get down to the troops and offload the needed equipment was to do the hover down. I could only see straight down through the chin bubble.

The instructors always told us from the time we began to hover to not look straight down because you couldn't detect you movement and hover height very well. Rather you were supposed to look out and pick something out a ways in front of the aircraft to focus on. Then you would slowly reduce the collective while maintaining directional control with the pedals and your position over the ground with the cyclic. That's the way you should do it, but when you are in a tight spot you need to deviate. I came to the high hover directly on top of the clearing of trees. I focused out front to make sure I was stopped and was headed as much into the wind as possible. I then looked down through the chin bubble and saw Billy Quinn who was to be my guide down through the trees.

Quinn, from New Jersey, was a squad leader at the time. I could see him through the chin bubble. Quinn was gonna guide me down. Now there are all kinds of standard hand and arm signals to communicate between the ground guide and the aircrew. Quinn didn't use any of them. I had to read his face and try to rely on the gestures he was making to tell me how close I was to hitting this tree or that tree. Little movements of his bent fingers told me to make very small movements. I would follow his directions and descend a bit, then look out front and check my position. My X-ray, and crew chief had eyeballs all around me and kept a constant chatter going about clearances right, rear and below the aircraft. The tedium continued until I finally got as low as I could go.

The area wouldn't let me set down. There were tree stumps of varying heights and positions. The skids were below the height of many of the stumps around us in the LZ. I suspect I was hovering no more than a foot or so above some small stumps, and the skids any more than a couple of feet off the ground. My tail was positioned just a few feet—laterally from the wreckage. I could see on Quinn's face where he wanted me, and how tight it really was. One mistake and there would be another wreck and with all the blades breaking off and stuff flying around there was a good chance I could kill a lot more. Quinn being right under me meant he would be one of the first to pay the price of my error.

He got me down to a hover about two feet in the air that put me about six inches to a foot above some of the stumps. The Blues came over and gently unloaded the cargo. I don't recall how many trips I made in there, but there were a few, and they didn't get any easier. We dropped off the maintenance team and they rigged the wreck for extraction. A CH-47 Chinook came in and took it out. The Blues improved the LZ making it a little easier this last time when we finally came in and pulled them all out.

I can still close my eyes and picture Quinn's face and his little hand gestures and finger pointing, guiding me down. None of the Blues injured in that episode came back to the troop.

I was to be married on Saturday, the 20th of April 1968 at Saint Helen's Roman Catholic Church in Howard Beach, New York. On the Wednesday before, I received a call at my Mom's home. The voice on the other end of the phone said, " Hey am I still invited to your wedding?" After all this time I heard Dave Bressam's voice on the other end of the phone. I was excited and almost in tears. He had remembered the date that Snooks and I had set. I said you bet and you're gonna stay at my house. Dave had lost an eye and had a leg injury that required him to wear a special spring apparatus that lifted his foot back to the horizontal. We had a good time together the day and night before the wedding. I haven't seen Dave since then. I had heard he had joined the peace movement and become quite active in seeking peace for Vietnam. I think he is a social worker in the Boston area.

Doc had been injured pretty badly too. Doc stayed in the Army after Vietnam. But his injuries were both physical and mental. He had lots of stress, and had trouble dealing with the reality of it all. I understand he finally checked himself out of this world.

Doc Haney standing in front of Blue lift ship named
Ol'Bullet. Doc was a well armed medic.

Going though some letters I had written home to my mother I came across one that gave her an advanced warning that a guy in the unit by the name of Billy Quinn was going home, and that he might give her a call. I don't remember if he ever called, but I do know he went home. I saw Billy at a reunion in Orlando, Florida in 1997. Billy is one of the good guys who will make it. I pray for Billy and all the other good guys.

Chapter Eleven

LZ Two Bits

Our move to LZ Two Bits on the Bong Son Plain wasn't really that much to talk about. Only a relatively short thirty or forty minute flight took us from the base camp, An Khe, to the LZ. Since this is where we first joined with the squadron, returning was almost like a homecoming. We weren't at Two Bits North as we had been in the past. Now we were on the south end of the north south runway. The area was obviously referred to as Two Bits South. We were located on some relatively level ground that was higher than the surrounding terrain of rice paddies. The troop area was shaped as a peninsula. When we arrived there was a concertina wire perimeter already established so we had some protection from the start. However it didn't satisfy our troop executive office, Major George Burrow who thought it not secure enough. He directed that the perimeter be beefed up with more wire.

We all got into the act of stringing some new wire around our area. Blues, pilots, crew chiefs—we all pitched in. Of course coming from the world of "helicopters and the CAV can do anything" perspective, in no time we started sling loading and unrolling the rolls of concertina wire from below a slick Huey into position on the perimeter. The Huey would stretch the wire from the previous coil and then all we had to do was tack it in with engineer stakes. It did speed the process up considerably. However, I don't think it would ever have been approved as a standard maneuver outside of the CAV.

All that remained was to lay and stake in the razor-sharp, tangle-foot wire, which was crisscrossed at about six inches above the ground. This made it impossible (supposedly) to run through the area between the rows of concertina, and even more difficult to crawl through the area as well.

Along the inside of the perimeter were placed engineer pre-pared bunkers that were built to specifications by the engineers The Blues and the crew chiefs pulled guard duty each night. Unfortunately the bunkers were hotter than hell to stay inside, so the Blues and crew chiefs would mostly sit and sleep on top of the bunkers rather than go inside.

At the junction between our area of the perimeter and the end of the runway area a Duster was positioned at night. The Duster was an old system that mounted quad 40mm guns on an open turret like pedestal. Each night the Duster would fire H&I rounds sporadically into the surrounding mountains and areas suspected of having the enemy. H&I was shorthand for Harass-ment and Interdiction Fires. These were meant to slow the enemy down on his nightly tasks. When the guns fired you would hear the heavy base thump-thump-thump-thump as each barrel fired its round. The 40mm is a slow round. So slow you could easily watch as the tracer and round went towards the hills and im-pacted.

The perimeter was manned from dusk to dawn each night with the enlisted men—the Blues, crew chiefs and the mechan-ics. The perimeter was further secured by periodic night patrols of Blues who would go out and set up ambushes to trap unknow-ing VC who attempted to get too close to the LZ.

Officers didn't pull guard or perimeter duty, though we did have assignments to go to certain bunkers as directed if the pe-rimeter was probed or attacked. We also pulled Officer of the Day (OD) duty. We would pull it according to a rotating duty roster the first sergeant would maintain; so we wouldn't get called that often at all.

Pulling OD did get interesting and hairy sometimes. As the OD you had to make mandatory rounds of the bunkers to ensure the bunkers were alert and properly manned. Also to make sure that anything observed was properly reported and passed on to the other bunkers. As the OD you wanted to be careful that you didn't get shot by a sniper as you walked from bunker to bunker. At the same time you didn't want to sneak up on a drowsy guard and startle him. To do so would certainly result in him firing his weapon at you before asking you for the password.

This happened in one of the other troops at LZ English. The young pilot snuck up to one bunker and jumped on top of it with a yell. The blue on duty wheeled about from his beach chair and stitched the guy with his M-16 rifle on full automatic. Word passed quickly of the incident and I for one took it very seriously. I didn't mind much getting killed by a bad guy too much, but from one of my own guys, I would really be pissed.

I decided that the sniper would have to get me. I would walk the perimeter making all sorts of noise to ensure the bunkers knew I was coming and also to keep them awake. On one night I stopped by and talked to the Duster crew. I was, still am, interested in Army equipment, and the Duster was really something to see. After some short talk with the crew they invited me to fire the damn thing. What a hoot! You sit in this little metal bucket type seat, almost like the seats on old farm tractors, and you fired the damn thing with your feet. The trigger was foot operated, thus leaving your hands free to point the weapon with hand cranks. Firing that gun was an absolute kick in the pants. Oh and I hit the target. That was easy; the target was the side of the hill. After firing 5 or so volleys, I thanked them and continued on my rounds.

Our perimeter stayed relatively quiet. Of course once someone saw or reported seeing something outside the perimeter everyone would begin seeing things. And should someone fire at something, the firing would spread all the way around the perimeter. We did have a couple of probes at Two Bits though. One night I recall some firing began along the line. We all reacted to the firing and made our way to the perimeter, as well we had a couple of guns launch to provide air cover. The XO (George Burrow) was "Johnny on the spot" at the perimeter, firing away with his 38-caliber pistol. He also threw a number of hand grenades at shadows in the wire. Throughout the night there was sporadic firing on the perimeter but nothing sustained. I don't think we took any damage to the aircraft or any of the tents, so the probe must have been a recon or we repelled the sappers.

If memory serves me correctly, they found a couple of bodies in the wire the next morning. One of which I was told, was one of the barbers who worked a chair outside the gate. Unlike our first time at Two Bits, I don't recall going into town or outside the gate. I think Top brought the barber in every day for us.

The Blues spent some time the next few days repairing the damage to the wire caused by the firing and the grenades. It is still amazing to me how anyone could get through all that wire.

I guess the toughest memory of the time at LZ Two Bits South was the loss of our Blue platoon leader Lou Porazzo. Lou was a scout pilot with the troop. He joined us in Duc Pho and was the life of the party. At Two Bits the scout pilot tent was alongside our Blue Lift tent and we really got to know one another. Since the gung-ho lieutenant we met on the C130 enroute to the Cav had spent his six months on the ground with the Blues the time came for him to go somewhere safer. LT Chilcote had served his time and he was reassigned as the rear detachment commander in An Khe. He was now responsible for the admin and tracking of incoming and out going personnel from the Troop. For whatever reason we hadn't gotten a replacement for Blue. The decision was made to rotate some of our officer pilots as the Blue platoon leader for a short two-month or so stint. Billy Johnson went first (I think.) Lou said he wanted the job next. I understand now that having ground troop experience on your record was an important thing for a real live officer when it came to promotion boards.

I don't think that is why Lou took the position; I think he wanted to lead the Blues after working on top of them for so long.

In any case Lou took over the Blues. What a wonderful thing to behold. The troops absolutely loved Lou Porazzo. And he loved them. The troops respected him, and he respected them in return. They all had fun and had it in the face of some really hard fighting and hard humping. The area of operations was a tough area. We systematically worked from the beach a la Apocalypse Now, and across the Bong Song plain, and all through and up the An Lao Valley.

I'll never forget one time flying Lou into a LZ. We turned final and the Blues as usual got out on the skids. All of a sudden I sensed something off to my left. I looked and here was Lou on the skid standing right next to my window looking in with a giant smile on his face. He moved back to the normal position just before jumping in with his Blues.

One day while working in the An Lao valley, the blues came under intense fire. The platoon was pinned down and they were trying to maneuver to flank the bad guys. The guns were providing air cover to the Blues. Lou was taking his squad down a gully when he was shot and fatally wounded. Blue India, Lou's radioman, transmitted the message that "Blue was hit and is dead." The news was not received well. The Blues wanted to kill everything in sight. Everyone wanted to kill everything in sight.

Some Blues thought the rounds came from one of our gunships; however that was shown to be wrong. What matters is that we lost a great guy, and great soldier and a great husband and father that day. When we moved north a few months later, we named the LZ we operated out of in his honor, LZ Porazzo just north of Tam Ky.

Years later I was proud and happy to learn that the 1st Cavalry Division had awarded one of its college scholarships to Lou's son. There was a picture of the son in the Saber, the Association's newspaper. Lou would have been proud of the son.

You've got to be shitting me? I don't know about you but sometimes I wonder about where some of these crazy ideas came from, and why they had to involve me and Jim.

One day at Duc Pho we were told our ship was gonna be rigged for some new thing that was gonna help us stop the bad guys from moving on the roads at night. Jim and I were put on night mission stand by. We went to our bird and saw them strapping this bundle of tubes—they looked like 2.75 rocket tubes from the guns but each tube was larger in diameter. The tube assemblies were being strapped in the seat well alongside the transmission wall, with the tubes oriented up and down, with the bottoms tilted out and away from the aircraft. The mouth of the tubes at the base had some kind of a release mechanism. Here's what we were supposed to do.

We were supposed to fly low level over the main highway at night with no lights on. An observer in the back of the aircraft with a night vision sight would search the road. When he saw the bad guys, obviously taking, or seeking cover, he would tell the operator who would pull the lanyards that opened the bottom of the tubes allowing the CS Gas grenades (who had their pins pulled as they went in the tubes) to fall to the ground. The gas would get to the bad guys causing them to get up and run. Then the gunship that was following us at altitude would kill them all.

The plan was similar to turning the kitchen light on at night in Brooklyn and catching all the roaches running all over the place. Only this time we were hoping to find the gooks making their way at night. Of course for safety sake Jim and I had to wear our gas masks throughout the operation. We flew that a few times. They had a problem with the damn canisters hanging up and not completely falling free. I think they went back to the drawing boards after that. I don't think we killed anyone on these missions. Thankfully we didn't kill ourselves either.

Sniffer Ship At Two Bits Jim and I were alerted that we would have something new installed on the bird. This time the 3/4 ton truck pulled up with a people sniffer machine. Here's what they did. The installed a little scoop which stuck out of my chin bubble. The scoop was attached to a vacuum cleaner type hose that stretched back to a little console type machine that an operator would look at. A little meter was affixed to the windscreen divider above the instrument panel. It had a needle which moved back and forth like a lie detector and had a couple of lights on it if I remember correctly.

Here's how this one worked. We were to fly low level again, but this time a little slower and we needed to fly a pattern based on the wind direction. We were supposed to orient and fly cross patterns 90 degrees from the direction of the wind. Gently working our way from downwind to upwind. The little scoop would capture a sample of the air. The sample would be tested for something in the air that only humans (and some types of monkeys) gave off. Based on the amount in the sample the lights would go on and the needle would deflect. The co-pilot would then mark the spot on his map or call the escorting gunbird so he could mark the location. At the end of the mission the plots would be given to intelligence and they would schedule artillery on them. As before, a gunship would follow at altitude and return fire if the bad guys decided to shoot at us, or to cover us in case the ship went down.

Our Huey with the Sniffer equipment installed. Photo
courtesy of Earl Hobbs

We flew that mission a lot. And not only at Two Bits, we flew
it all the way up through Camp Evans in March of 1968. Jim and
I never received any fire on these missions, though Mike Covey
took hits twice flying the mission. He took one in Jim's bird, and
right before I left he took one in the oil cooler of my ship "Baby
Snooks II."

We also made a training film—no kidding—on the use of the
sniffer. We never saw the final product but Jim did find a still
picture in the Washington Archives they took of us during the
filming. We were posed in front of Troop Operations at Two Bits
looking at a map that Jim was holding. To be sure the audience
knew what we were doing Jim had drawn a large goose egg on the
map and labeled it "SNIFFER" in big block letters.

Jim even got to see his brother because of the Sniffer. Jim
took the machine and the operator and went to the Navy (where
his brother just happened to be serving) and flew with them for a
week. His head has yet to return to normal dimensions since this
stardom.

On one of our sniffer flights we took an army photographer
with us. He was a still picture cameraman. He was sitting on the

right side of the aircraft as we worked the hills alongside the An Lao Valley. This was really fun. Because you would fly low level, fast, and climb up a draw, as you reached the peak or top of the hill you find yourself up in the air over the valley. You would have to bottom the pitch to try to stay at tree top level. This resulted in a feeling similar to a roller coaster, when you leave your stomach momentarily. Well I had my trusty Super 8 movie camera cranking away as Jim flew. Just as we hit the top of the hill and Jim was descending to capture the tree top again, I heard someone yell "SHIT!" from the back. The voice came from the Sniffer operator who looked as though he was trying to shake something off his right arm. I quickly turned and saw suspended in the air in front of the photographer's face a formless blob of vomit. It stayed there as we went weightless; and then, as gravity caught up, the blob descended all over the Photographer. I captured the guy's face right after he realized and experienced being doused with his own vomit. I guess this was the second round of vomit, the first one had elicited the "SHIT" comment from the Sniffer operator who had caught part of the first round. I want everyone to remember, Jim was flying when the guy got sick.

Complying with the rules for etiquette of flight, the cameraman cleaned up the mess when we landed.

Crop Dusting One day at Two Bits a 3/4 ton truck showed up and they started strapping a liquid tank in our bird. Then they attached a long spray bar that extended fifteen of so feet out each door. Our mission this time was to fly up the sides of the mountain which formed the An Lao Valley. When we found the little rice paddies cut into the side of the hills we were to hover around the paddy and spray the stuff in the tank. This was a defoliant. Was it Agent Orange? I don't know. They didn't tell us and we didn't ask.

Huey equipped with the tank and boom to spray
defoliant on remote rice paddies. Photo Courtesy of
Earl Hobbs

All I know is we went out there and found the little paddies
and sprayed them good. We would come back from those mission drenched with the oily-like smelly substance that had back
sprayed into the cockpit and literally cover the aircraft. Oh course
we had the obligatory gunship at altitude in case we got shot at or
down.

I don't know how many days we did that. But we did it a
bunch of times. We never took fire or took a hit either. However
knowing that you were spraying Charlie's own private garden
and that if he opened fire you would surely be shot down in the
middle of a one ship LZ made the mission hairy. If you were shot
down it would be quite a while before anyone could reasonably
get to you.

Phu Cat I don't know what the reason was, perhaps some
intelligence estimate or something. All I know is that for a period
of time, we used to have to take a few of our aircraft to the Air
Force Base at Phu Cat each night. We would go to Phu Cat before
last light and return to Two Bits shortly after first light. I don't
know why, and I was not about to complain. The Air Force knew

how to live. Nice quarters, real beds, clean sheets, great club, real showers, and flush toilets!

Whenever we went to and Air Force Base they always had great quarters. Except that they had separate facilities for the officers and enlisted. As a CAV crew we didn't really see this distinction as being too important. We carried an extra fatigue shirt with wings and WO rank for the crew chief so they could come to the club and stay in officer country.

The Air Force pilots were pretty good guys too. I don't know how they did it but they had telephones in their rooms and would let us use them. The system wasn't exactly Ma Bell, but it allowed you to hear a familiar voice half way around the world. The calls were actually part of the MARS (Military Amateur [?] Radio) system. MARS consisted of a network of HAM radio operators who would pick up the skip wave and relay it to an operator close to your destination and then make the final telephonic connection. I was interesting all right. When you finished your sentence, you would have to say "over." That signaled the other party to begin speaking. Ending their point with, "over." Making MARS calls was an interesting activity for me I can only imagine how Snooks felt about the system.

I have learned that B Troop had worked out of Phu Cat before they went to Two Bits the first time. Maybe that's why we went back there. You know, as a WO1 helicopter pilot we really didn't know much about anything other than how to fly the aircraft. If the bad guys ever captured us and asked about plans or military operations I couldn't tell them anything because I didn't know anything.

A few years ago I was talking to another B Troop alumnus who had also retired from the Army. He was a Captain in B Troop, and retired as a full colonel (O-6). He was working as a civilian with training systems and was reviewing some brigade or battalion order to be used in the training session. He asked me if I had ever seen an order in B Troop. I told him I hadn't, except that I did see some battle reports that Bert had written when he was in operations at Chu Lai. He replied that he didn't think we ever had one. Then he began asking about how and where we were taught how to fight the Troop. This was another tale of superior performance by the leadership of the 1/9th in how they quickly passed on the tactics techniques and procedures from mouth to ear, from veteran to FNG. And how well it worked. You see someone was always in charge in the air. When one team left to refuel another team came on station and was briefed over the radio in a very short time. When the aircraft in charge went down the wingman took over, and stayed in charge until he went for fuel or Six (the troop commander) came on station. The smoothness of the handoff and the economy of chatter and discussion, particularly in the very fluid and fast changing conditions of each fight is truly amazing. I wonder to myself these days about all the emphasis on planning and orders and coordination, etc. needed for a unit to go to fight. And all we did was go out and find the bad guys and kill them before they killed us. I don't think we would have been any better with the command and control stuff available today.

July 1967—A tough month for Blue 39 and 39X-ray.

Breaking Off the Approach Blue 39 was the callsign for WO1 Jim Pratt the aircraft commander who flew the slot (last in the formation) for B Troop, 1/9 CAV, in Vietnam for most of 1967 and the beginning of 1968. X-rays were the pilots who flew as second in command to the aircraft commanders. 39 x-ray was me, WO1 John Flanagan. I had come to B Troop in April 1967 as my first assignment out of flight school. After flying with each of the aircraft commanders in the platoon as was customary for a FNG (F*cking New Guy), I settled in as 39 X-ray. Jim and I had a great relationship right from the start, but that's another story. Suffice to say our relationship began in VN carried on back in the states, and continues to this day.

Jim and I flew together each day. One day in early July 1967 we were flying in our normal slot position on a combat assault into a hilltop LZ 3/4ths of the way into the An Lao Valley. Turning final over the valley floor, we went to a trail formation and took up spacing between the aircraft to allow for the single ship LZ that was on the south side of the valley. The technique here was to land the four ships one at a time in the LZ as quickly as possible. That is to minimize the time between the first and last ship's delivery of the Blues.

As the first ship was about to land we noticed that our controls began to stiffen up. Sensing an emergency due to a failure in our hydraulics system, Jim made the radio call that we were breaking off the approach and returning to base. In fact, the hydraulics did fail. The hydraulic systems in the Huey acted like power steering works in your car. With it operational and functioning as designed, moving the aircraft controls was a finger tip operation; without it, it feels like a hundred tons of effort is required to move the controls a bit.

We told the crewchief to brief the blues on what was happening and to tell them to fasten their seat belts. Our Blues never used the seat belts. When we would turn final our Blues would stand on the skids of the aircraft and jump off the bird before we could touch down. There were few occasions we ever touched down in an LZ. In fact we were lucky on this day for we sensed the hydraulics problem before they got on the skids. It would have been a bit trickier to get them back inside the aircraft during the go-around. We told the crewchief to tell them we were going to make a slow low approach to a running landing to the runway. And, that we would be sliding down the runway until we stopped, and then once we stopped they should un-ass the bird straight out the sides to get clear.

We stayed at altitude on the way back to LZ Two Bits, on the Bong Song plain. Jim and I reviewed the checklist, discussed the procedures we were going to follow, and what we would do in the event the various things that could go wrong, did. Calling the tower we stated our condition gave the complete report, tail number, callsign, fuel on board, time remaining, souls on board, etc. We tried to keep our voices, deep, strong, calm, confident and controlled, but knew they were a few octaves higher than normal.

Earlier that month or the month before, we had seen an ARA bird that had lost his tail rotor attempt a running landing at Two Bits like Jim and I were preparing to do. This guy had done a great job preparing for the landing. It looked like his tail rotor drive shaft had failed because the tail rotor blades were was just freewheeling like a pinwheel or a windmill in a mild breeze. The pilot maintained directional control by maintaining enough forward airspeed to allow the airframe to streamline. If you get too slow you lose the streamlining and the aircraft begins to spin in the opposite direction of the main rotor blades—there goes another physics lesson "for every action there is an opposite and equal reaction."

In preparation for the landing the pilot had flown low over the river and jettisoned the pilot and copilot's doors, and jettisoned his two twenty-four round rocket pods. He then flew around and burned most of his fuel off. He then came in on a shallow approach to a running landing. The exact same maneuver Jim and I were faced with.

He touched down nicely and was doing real good until he began to slow down as he was skidding down the runway. We could see the rotor disc begin to tilt as he attempted to maintain directional control and keep the aircraft from turning sideways. Then it began that right turn about halfway down the runway. Almost imperceptible at first, then just a little, then growing tighter and faster, until finally the aircraft was almost 90 degrees to the runway. Then it happened. Just as you thought he was going to stop, and make it. The left skid caught the ground and the aircraft began to roll over. Mesmerized I thought I was watching this in slow motion. The main rotor tilted way down as the fuselage started to go up. More and more of the top of the cabin and the tail boom could be seen, as the rotors contacted the ground and the aircraft rolled over. Kicking up dust and dirt, and debris all over the place. And the Huey was sitting there rolling over with the blades just beating the helicopter into the ground. The crash crew was right there and there was no fire as I recall. I believe the crew escaped without any major injuries. But man I'll always remember the sight of that bird slowly rolling over and beating itself into submission. That guy had done what appeared to be correct right up till the time he rolled over. Little did I know our turn was to come shortly.

Our emergency was different from his, and less serious. We still had our tail rotor and flight controls operating, we knew it would take both of us working together to move them to maintain stable flight.

We requested the crash crew be standing by for us. When cleared to land we began a gentle descent, minimizing the amount and the number of control movements, trying to keep things as normal as possible. Jim and I had practiced doing things together and now that practice was paying off.

We would sometimes even hover around with one of us on the cyclic and collective, and the other working the pedals, and all the other combinations. We used to challenge each other on our pilot technique by seeing who could make a landing with the least amount of changes and smallest amount of control movement. We got to be pretty good working as one body, flying the aircraft. Today was going to be a test of how well we could really do.

We swung into a gentle turn and lined up on the runway heading towards the south. We slowed to approach speed, then slowed some more to just enough to keep our forward movement to help streamline the aircraft as we tried to lower the collective as we came over the runway's threshold. We had set up a nice low angle approach, probably not more than 2 or 3 degrees. We crossed over the threshold and everything was going fine, but now for the intense part, the last few feet. The last inch or two of the getting the collective down and the aircraft the last few feet to the ground was rough. Jim and I were both lock armed onto the collective and straining against the seatbelt with our bodies trying to get enough force to push the collective down. As we went by the tower I remember seeing the fire truck just off our right rear side chasing us down the runway. I also caught a glimpse of one of the tower operators hanging out of the tower cab with his Super 8mm-movie camera. Guess he didn't want to miss the excitement.

Finally, we made contact with the runway—very gently I might add—now if we can just get this thing stopped without rolling over or running off the end of the runway. We skidded and skidded as we struggled to get the collective all the way down, and we were almost standing on the pedals to keep the nose straight and keep us from rolling over.

Well, just past our turn off to B Troop's parking area on the southwest side of the runway we came to a stop. When finally stopped the aircraft sort of rocked forward a bit, and then came to a complete stop. I quickly turned my head to tell the Blues to leave but they were gone before I could say anything.

What did surprise me was the firefighter running towards me with a hose pointed directly at me. I waved frantically, and shouted "No! NO!"

Jim didn't know what I was yelling about, he just hastened shutting down the aircraft. Before turning the radios off we called the tower, gave them a thumbs up report—"No fire, no injury"—and thanked them for the help. The tower told us to hover the aircraft clear of the runway. We said "No we've had enough, thank you," and shut the radios off and walked to OPs. Our maintenance officer, WO1 Larry Koler, met us as we were walking away and went to the aircraft. Minutes afterwards he ground taxied the broke bird clear of the runway. Not a smart thing to do, but that's why maintenance officers get paid all that extra money.

The maintenance inspection showed we had blown a hydraulic line inside the hell hole and lost all of our hydraulics by the time we got back to Two Bits. Hydraulic fluid smells really awful when it really heats up. I can still smell it in my mind today.

Dog POL Later that same month Jim and I had returned to Two Bits from an ash and trash mission to An Khe, the First Air Cavalry's base camp. Ash and trash flights referred to those administrative flights where we picked up mail, parts and stuff like that. After offloading we had to refuel. Our refueling point was further north on the Bong Song plain. A place called Dog POL (petroleum, oil and lubricants), adjacent to LZ English.

A short flight of only six or so miles north was needed to reach the POL point. We were flying at our customary low level—tree top level—when the big yellow master caution light on the instrument panel lit up! The big yellow master caution light tells you that something isn't right and you should look at the master caution panel on the radio console situated on the pedestal between the two pilots. The master caution panel on the pedestal has about twenty or so segments which can be individually illuminated. These tell the pilot which of the systems or part of the system that is malfunctioning. When we lost the hydraulics earlier in the month the big yellow light came on and the hydraulic pressure segmented light lit up.

This time when I looked down I read the light to Jim "Left Fuel Boost Pump Out."

Jim, acknowledged my reading, by saying "Yep, I'm starting my climb right now."

Before we could feel the climb begin, the big yellow master caution light came on again. This time we both read it aloud "Right Fuel Boost Pump Out." I said, 'Oh shit, all we have left is the engine driven pump left."

In a Huey, you need something to pump fuel to her engine. As long as she had fuel, the Huey was pretty happy. Now with the two electrically driven pumps out, we had to relay on the mechanically driven, engine fuel pump. Without it, the engine would quit. Only rarely would you expect to lose the engine driven pump, but hell losing both boost pumps at the same time wasn't common either.

Jim, responded "Yeah I'm picking a spot now." He was referring to selecting an emergency touchdown landing area if we have to put it down deadstick. One of the key selection criteria for landing is that you land into wind. Our luck, we were heading north with a tail wind. If we are to land we will have to do a 180-degree turn. As Jim continued to climb to get some altitude so we could make a safe turn into the wind, I tried to find the problem, we still had plenty of fuel showing on the gauge, and none of the circuit breakers had popped.

From the time the first master caution light came on until now, about 20 seconds has elapsed. Now 20 seconds from the first light, the third master caution light, with the dreaded segmented warning light announcing "Engine Driven Pump Out' light, came on. It got real quiet from the engine quitting, and exciting, as Jim racked us into a hard right turn into the wind, and noisy as I yelled into the radio on the tower frequency "Maydaymaydaymayday, SaberBlue39goingdown3southofDog." Midway in the turn I looked back and saw our crewchief Tankersley working feverishly trying to buckle his seat belt. I heard the tower come back with a "roger" to my transmission and saying that my OPs is being alerted.

Jim did a great job cranking that aircraft around back into the wind. We touched down with the heal of the right skid first as it plowed through the top of a soft (thank God) muddy rice paddy dike. The left skid hit next and then we stopped in the middle of the rice paddy.

As we came to rest, I looked back just in time to see Tank get the buckle closed. Now he had to unsnap it.

Jim did a great job doing a 180 autorotation into a wet and muddy rice paddy but now we had other things to do since we were sitting in the middle of a rice paddy with a small group of huts less than a thousand meters away. I got a radio call to OPs on our FM radio telling them we were down with no fire, and no injuries. They advised a pink team had launched and the Blues were on the way.

Now we were alone in the paddy—Jim, Tank and me. We were far enough away from the villages and the huts to observe if anyone was going to come out after us. This was an area we flew over a lot and never got shot at, but we had also made some sweeps where the Blues had found some of the bad guys. And you never knew what was really going to happen. We sort of crouched down oriented towards the huts and the tree line. We didn't have much time to worry though, the most beautiful sight in the world appeared within 3 minutes of us going down.

First the scout team, then our three sister ships with Blues standing on the skids were on final approach to the paddy. With a pink team providing cover. They got off the aircraft, and we got on. Happy? You bet! We were flown back to Two Bits and began filling out the reports. No we didn't run out of gas. Really we didn't.

Our maintenance officer, WO1 Larry Koler, flew out with the maintenance team to see what was wrong. Everyone was certain we ran out of fuel. Larry inspected the aircraft, cranked it and without adding any fuel checked her out and flew her home.

Later maintenance found out what had happened was the scavenger pumps weren't working. And since Jim and I were flying nose low, the fuel couldn't get to the boost pumps so they quit. Then with no fuel the engine driven pump went out. It took some strong words and a lot of work, but maintenance found the problem.

That's two for July, but we still had some month to go.

Jim and I had a lot to talk about so far that month.

Jet Aces Coming back from another ash and trash run to An Khe we dropped off our passengers and went to LZ Dog and refueled. Now, between LZ Dog and LZ Two Bits was a neat little river that wound its way through the plain to the South China Sea. Most times when you came back from Dog and had nothing to do, we would run the river. That is fly down it at high speed and low level. Not smart, but a lot of fun.

The river also had a couple of bridges that crossed over, which provided a very large challenge to many a young helicopter pilot. A number of aircraft had ended up in the river after some pilot accepted the challenge. Jim and I would never do anything as foolish as that. We talked about it and sized it up a couple of times but calculated the chance for success not as great as the chance for disaster. And the way the cards were being dealt for us, we didn't need to go looking for certain disaster.

This afternoon, we decided to not run the river, but rather fly directly back so we didn't miss chow. The mess tent was going to close any minute now.

Arriving at our unit area we decided to park up on the gun platoon's revetments because they were closer to the mess tent. The idea was park here and eat. Then, after dinner, we would move it back to our ramp. No sweat.

I was hovering the helicopter into the revetment when at once a strong metallic "thunk" was heard, the aircraft began a turn to the right, and my left peddle wouldn't work. Recognizing no pedal control caused by a tail rotor failure I cut the throttle immediately as I said "shit." The idea is that by cutting the engine removes the torque and the turn will stop. You should be able to gently settle to the ground.

Works in practice all the time. This time however, the turn didn't slow or stop quick enough. The nose of the aircraft was dropping in an unusual nose low and uneven angle. Before we hit the revetment and rolled over upside down I planted the collective. Luckily that prevented us from rolling over. Man what noise! Man what a jolt! Ripping of metal, a high screeching whine of the turbine. I looked out my left window and thought I saw fire. The air was fiery red to my left and looked like a combination of flames and heavy smoke. I didn't smell any smoke though. In reality the sand from the revetment's sandbags were thrown up in the air from the main rotor blades striking them. The setting sun turned the air red.

The crew chief popped my door open, I started to get out, but had to sit down again and unbuckle my seat belt. Not able to fit between the seat armor which was locked in the forward position and the doorjamb, I went through the plating; breaking the fasteners that hold the wing to the seat. I went directly over the hill and sought cover from what I knew was going to be one hell of an explosion. Not hearing one I looked up after a time and saw lots of the members of my unit running towards the accident. I met up with Jim at the back of this group and went towards the aircraft.

What a sight! There was our bird, sitting on the ground with its rear end slid off its cross tubes, no tail rotor, no main rotor blades—nothing turning at all—, and the engine screaming as it continued running at 6600 rpm with no load on it at all. In fact even the big, five foot tall transmission assembly was ripped out of the bird and thrown about twenty feet into the revetment. We got back to the aircraft and shut down the engine.

The story doesn't end there however. The most seriously damaged gunship was placed at the end of our ramp sitting alongside our bird. Both of them had been rigged for evacuation by the big tandem rotor Chinook helicopter. The Hook came in and descended and "sat" on the gun bird as it attempted to hook up the load. This caused the Huey to slip off the aft cross tubes. Looking at the two Hueys, with each slid off its cross tubes in opposite directions, they appeared to be gigantic surreal bookends.

The tail rotor failure occurred on 29 July. The commander gave Jim and me off for the rest of the month. I guess three is really a charm. The scout platoon kept inviting Jim and me to park in their area. There were rumors that scout pilot Jere "Fat Albert" Anderson was taking up a collection to encourage us to park in their area. I guess they figured if we crashed again we would probably wipe out their entire platoon and they would get a few days off.

Chapter Twelve

Chu Lai

Captain Burnham called us together late one afternoon and alerted us that we were to saddle up and move out
within the next 24 or 48 hours. We were going up north again to
I Corps to a place called Chu Lai. Chu Lai he told us was north of
Duc Pho and South of Da Nang. That night all the pilots received
map sheets for the new area. I remember all of us in the mess
tent trying to cut and paste and acetate all the map sheets together for our new AO (area of operations). First you had to trim
the edges of each individual map sheet. Then you would carefully align them, ensuring the contour lines and grid lines lined
up, then you would scotch tape them on the backside to keep
the sheets together. Then, on the front side, before you put the
acetate on, you would plot (locate by grid coordinates) all the
firebases and permanent LZs using the coordinates you had
scribbled down hastily in your notebook during the briefing. After plotting the LZ you would then attempt to cover the maps with
acetate. I was never any good at taping or wrapping presents
either. I guess being poor we didn't get much practice in wrapping things. In any case I always had trouble putting the maps
together without obliterating several major terrain features, or
capturing large amounts of air bubbles which would cause creases
and hide or distort some of the map features. Given the bad light-

ing, the lateness of the hour and my general poor attitude that evening, I was amazed that I got my maps together at all that night.

After we got our maps finished we crashed in our cots till morning. We went to bed late that night, and rose early the next morning. Everyone was in a hurry to tear down the camp and finish packing for the move. Being in an airmobile unit made moving a little more convenient because we didn't have much to move, but the day was still filled with loading, flying, unloading, refueling and then doing it again.

Light rain fell on the windscreens as we left Two Bits and flew north along the coast below the low clouds. Windshield wipers weren't used very often because they would scratch the Plexiglas windshield making it difficult to see though when the sun was shining. The rain streamlined across the windshield as we flew a loose formation to our new home.

Chu Lai was not prepared for the arrival of the Cavalry. We were assigned an area on the bare beach to the southeast side of the base. There wasn't anything there at all except rain and wind. We spent the first night sleeping in the aircraft. The next day we put the tents up and began to dig in. We also started flying missions that day though at a reduced rate. While we improved the positions and flew the CO continued to press for more suitable accommodations. We were used to sleeping in tents, being on the perimeter, and all that. But before so were all the other folks. Here, however the Marines had, real buildings as Bachelor Officers Quarters (BOQ's), and even officer's clubs. By contrast all we had was sand and rain.

Then the weather turned really foul. A typhoon approached the coast and we were getting the hell beat out of us. The ol'man, Major Lew Beasley had some harsh words with the Marine in charge of the base. Beasley found an empty hanger and threatened to shoot the lock off the building, so the base commander allowed us to spend the next few nights in the hanger. Walking into the hanger, we looked like refugees with our sleeping bags and duffel bags lined up all over the floor. We were pretty close to the Marine Air Wing Officer's Club, so that almost made up for the nights on the beach. I don't remember how many nights we spent there. That time is a blur to me. I do remember the fun we had at the clubs. Finally we were assigned space on the northeast point of Chu Lai.

For the first time since joining B Troop our living quarters had real floors and real walls and a real corrugated metal roof instead of tent canvass. The furniture remained early-tour rocket box fabrications. Given a couple of 2.75 rocket boxes you could make a pretty dandy writing table by setting one horizontally and attaching vertical legs made from the wood from the other box. Comm wire is double strand light wire that is used to connect military telephones and radios. We used some commo wire to hold the lid of the top box in a flat position for the tabletop. When you left the tent you could still fold the lid up and close the box to protect your mail and writing paper from the blowing sand, dirt and wind.

Not everyone had these hooches however. The area that we were in was divided by our aircraft's parking and landing area. Most of the officers were in the hooches on one side of this postage stamp size helipad, while the remaining officers and the enlisted men lived in tents on the other side. The operations tent, mess hall, and supply were on the other side too. It wasn't that far from one side to the other really, but we weren't as close to the Blues as we were before.

At Chu Lai we had access to a real PX, and two real Officers Clubs. One was the Marine Air Wing Club alongside the main runway, the other club belonged to Task Force Oregon (who later would become the Americal Division) Club. Since the Task Force Oregon club was just a short walk up the hill from our area we frequented that club more often.

Each morning we would load up and launch at the break of day up to a forward laager area—LZ Porazzo, a base for one of the mechanized units. They had tanks and armored personnel carriers (APCs). (The LZ was named after LT Lou Porazzo, who was killed in the An Lao Valley while leading the Blue Platoon.) We would launch recon teams all day, one after the next, launching the Blues on endless search-and-destroy and sweep missions. Aircraft shoot downs kept us busy. The LZ had a sand-bagged walled, two-room operations bunker, two—two-hole shitters, and some ammo boxes we shaped into a table. The aircraft and the bunker were the only break from the sun and the weather.

B Troop Huey Hog coming over the wire and passing a tank at LZ Porazzo. Photo courtesy of Jim Pratt

Photo shows B Troop aircraft laagering at Porazzo. An armored personnel carrier can be seen in the upper right of the photo. Photo courtesy of Jim Pratt

Entering from the sunlight the bunker's darkness made it almost impossible to see. A wooden bench was attached all around the perimeter of the room. The operations officer ran the troop tactical operations center in the second room. The main focus of this room was a large map on the wall and a set of loud radios that blared with the chatter of our crews as they performed their recons.

My brother-in-law Bill, doing his part for the war effort carefully removed the centerfold from each of his extensive collection of Playboy magazines and sent them to me. I donated them to the troop, and with the help of Jim Pratt and some of the other guys, we wall papered the first room of the bunker. When we finished we had a work of art, which provided us all some much-needed distraction during the endless hours of waiting.

Flying out to LZ Porazzo every morning we had to remember that some folks—the tankers—lived there at night and the perimeter was to be considered "hot." This point was drilled into us repeatedly when, coming in low across the perimeter wire on an approach and keying the FM radio caused some of the claymore mines positioned in the defensive perimeter wire to explode. The first few times this happened to us we thought that the tankers were firing the claymores at us on purpose. Only later did we learn to not only to coordinate with the ground troops to remind them to disarm the mines at first light, but for us to also stay off the damn FM radio when crossing the wire on landing.

The tankers provided another distraction. They would come over to see the holes in our aircraft and we would go over to see the remains of their APCs that had unfortunately hit a land mine. We would also give some of their guys a ride back to the PX or help them get out of there on emergency leave home.

It also provided an opportunity to screw off. I got a chance to drive my first tank at LZ Porazzo in 1967. Little did I know that three years later while on my second tour in Vietnam I would receive a direct commission from Chief Warrant Officer 2 (CWO2) to 1st Lieutenant of Armor. I got in the driver's compartment and the tank commander showed me where the controls were—gas, brake, and steering bar—and then he got in the turret and said, "let's go." I drove around the area for a couple of minutes then I saw the berm by the firing pit where we test fired our small arms weapons. I asked the TC if we could climb the berm. He said no problem and coached me over the top. I was sold that from that moment on that tanks were neat.

Of course turn about was fair play and on a couple of chow runs back to Chu Lai the guy in the copilot's seat would be a tanker getting his first flight lesson. I guess we shouldn't have done either of those things, but when you're 21 and invincible, things happen.

After a hard day of doing what we did, we would return to the safety and security of Chu Lai and try to forget the day.

Forgetting the day usually involved a visit to the club. At first we went to the Marine club almost exclusively. Later when the other club opened we went to the MAW once or twice a week.

One good thing about the MAW you got to meet some of the Marine pilots who were performing bombing missions over the north. Getting to know them we learned that they sometimes returned with undelivered ordnance which they had to jettison over the South China Sea before recovering at Chu Lai. It wasn't long before some of the MAW guys had our operations frequency and would call us if they had some bombs left over. Upon hearing them call, Six would coordinate an ad hoc air strike in support of our operations. Much better use of our taxes bombing the bad guys then drowning the bombs in the sea.

I don't know if this was also something we shouldn't have done, but we did. Another feature of this camaraderie was that sometimes when our flight was loitering waiting for an insertion or enroute, a Marine F4 with flaps fully extended, gear hanging out, flying at the edge of a stall, would try to join the Blue flight formation. They could never get slow enough, nor could we get fast enough to really call it a formation flight, but we had fun, and some of the Blues had some great photo opportunities.

Que Son Valley 1967 I remember a lot of stuff about my time in B Troop, 1st of 9th Cavalry, in Vietnam in 1967 and 1968. But I don't remember all of the details, or all of the parts of the various episodes. One such incident occurred while we were up in Chu Lai and working out of a forward laager area LZ Porazzo. I don't know how it all got started, it could have been a radio call onto OPs from a team on station over some grunts, or it could have been a call from OPs to me while I was enroute someplace else. In any case I was flying, I think Jack craft was my x-ray, and had a crew chief on board. I don't remember if the CE was Dale Dungan or SP5 Art Dunn. I think Dale was with me. In any case, there were just the three of us on board.

We were called to an area just west of LZ Ross at the mouth of the Que Son Valley. I think Rick Harris was flying the gunship in the area and called us in. I got the briefing over UHF radio from the white bird that was working over a grunt unit who was trying to move back out of the valley. The situation as I recall being told was that the unit had come under some pretty intense contact and taken a bunch of casualties. So many wounded, and as I recall about 8 or 10 KIA. White Bird said he was having trouble getting a Medevac in to pull out the dead and wounded.

A note here: some of the medical units, we were told, had been restricted from landing in hot LZs, which meant that there couldn't have been any rounds fired in the last thirty minutes. I don't remember them landing in the LZ that day. I could be wrong about this, but I don't remember.

The LZ was a one ship opening with the approach axis east to west. A stream cut across the eastern side of the LZ. The trees and the terrain made it a confined area, with the west, or stream-side having the lowest obstacles. The enemy was to the west, and close. The wind was not strong but, as luck would have it, coming from the west.

Normal procedures would require the approach and take off be from east to west, into the wind. And the more loaded the aircraft, the more important wind direction was. The fact that the enemy was close and to the west presented a problem of how to get in and get out without getting shot to shit on the way out. I did a quick look at the LZ and told the white bird I was going to try an approach from east to west. I went in and set down in the LZ—something we in B Troop didn't do very often.

The troops looked like they had been through a lot—and they had. I remember the crew chief who always sat behind me on the left side of the aircraft was out on the ground on the right side of the aircraft trying to get the seats pulled up so we could lay the casualties on the floor. I gave my x-ray the controls, and I climbed between our seats to help unlock the seats and strap them up. The other bodies were being placed on the left side of the aircraft. The doors were shut so they wouldn't roll out on the flight back. This was strange, because we always had the doors pinned open. The time on the ground seemed like an eternity, but was probably no more than two, maybe three minutes. I think we were in contact with the enemy firing in the western area. I called the white bird and told him I was coming out backwards—to the east, the same way I came in. I picked the bird up to a hover, and began a right pedal turn as I continued to apply collective to gain some altitude so I would just miss the vegetation to the east. I wanted to stay low so the bad guys in the west couldn't get a line of sight on me. We went directly to LZ Ross, dropped the causalities off at the Medevac pad. I went back to the LZ.

I saw the Medevac bird in an orbit above and to the east of the LZ at altitude. There were only bodies left to be extracted and Medevac could only pull out WIAs. I went back in. This time I remember, and see it clearly. Two soldiers carrying a pole on their shoulders, with a comrade tied to it as one might carry an animal after a successful hunt. I can see the face on the dead soldier today. The stark look of death, frozen on the pained, surprised dirty and sweaty face. A young soldier about my age (20) or a little younger, perhaps. More dead came behind the first. When the doors were shut and we were ready to come out again I glanced back and the bird looked full. I couldn't distinguish how many, but the compartment was full. And the smell! I will never forget the distinct smell of dead men.

In B Troop we always carried the same the Blues everyday. And the nature of the work was typically a series of insertions, sweep a village, or sweep an area, extract the Blues, and then insert them again at a new location. I always carried extra "stuff" on board for the Blues. In the LZ I motioned one of the grunts over to my side and handed him a bunch of the stuff, a carton of cigarettes, some sacks of candy, stuff from the sundry packs of goodies. The grunt took them with a confused blank stare. He didn't understand. I didn't understand either. Until I thought about it. I was trying to help them, tell them I cared, and all I had to give them were these cigarettes, and that candy.

As we returned to the Medevac pad, I asked the crewchief

how many we had back there. He told me he couldn't count them—"they are piled like cordwood back here," he said.

I brought them to the Medevac pad. The medics did not want to accept the KIAs. I was supposed to take them someplace else. Graves registration is where I think they said. I don't know if I drew my gun and told them to take them and make sure they're dead, or if I just threatened to shoot them if they didn't take them. I remember being out of the aircraft nose to nose with someone. I do know the soldiers were taken off my bird and carried up to the aid station and lined up outside as someone—someone with a stethoscope around their neck—went from body to body checking them.

We took off, went to refuel, and reported via fox mike (FM radio) to operations that we were clear and enroute from refuel and then returning to the LZ Porazzo. Operations called back and diverted us to Chu Lai for the chow run. We picked up the cooks and the mermite container containing lunch and flew them to LZ Porazzo. I couldn't eat lunch that day; and the smell of the dead remained in the aircraft for me for a least a week.

Those grunts and the white bird that found a way to help the grunts are the heroes of this tale. They got caught in the valley and had to fight their way back carrying and caring for their comrades.

I could be mistaken. Maybe the Medevac did pull some of the guys out. In any case, this should not be taken as a criticism of the Medevac crews who had to follow the orders they were given by their medical commanders.

George Burrow—LZ Porazzo—1967 MAJ George Burrow after having been the B Troop, 1/9 Cavalry executive officer was placed in command of the Troop when the former commander's (MAJ Lewis Beasley) replacement was evacuated within a few weeks of assuming command.

While we lived at Chu Lai, we worked out of a forward laager LZ Porazzo. During this period we were in a series of daily high contacts. Burrow was out there in his glory, riding to the sounds of the guns. So much so it appeared that the Division CG was with us every other day pinning another impact DFC or Silver Star on George or one of the guys. George was always in the thick of things, and of course accounted for attracting more of his share of enemy fire, accumulating lots of hits to his aircraft, and leaving more than a couple in the rice paddies—sometimes more than one a day! I think George was shot down 13 times during his tour with us.

The effect of these actions included him receiving Plexiglas damage to his eyes, which required his constant use of eye drops. George would come into the bunker at Porazzo, sit in his beach chair and hand me his eye drops. I would squirt his eyes, one by one, and he would go on with his business of monitoring the fight. Depending on the length of his stay on the ground, I would do it again before his next flight. I don't know why he asked me to do this for him. I never did see him ask anyone else to do it. George, now a retired full colonel (06), told me he couldn't see out of that eye for a long time back then.

This isn't much of a war story for the 1st of the 9th Cavalry. It is a small thing that I remember. I remember thinking about what the flight surgeon might say about this; and how this might affect his flying. But ya know, I really didn't care. I had confidence in this leader and this pilot. And I knew that he wouldn't do anything to jeopardize the unit or his crew. I also learned about personal sacrifice, and individual valor from him.

13 November—A Day To Remember

13 November 1967.

Chu Lai.

It started out just like any other day at Chu Lai with the first light flight to LZ Porazzo.

In the morning we were out doing Hawk Flights. A hawk flight is where a white bid (The scout), a red bird (The Gunship), and a blue bird (a lift bird with 4 or 5 infantry) go out into the area of operations together sampling the population. The white bird under the protective eyes of the red bird would seek out suspicious looking indigenous persons working in the fields or traveling on the trails, paths or dikes. Once identified the blue bird would be called in to insert the Blues and pick up the suspicious person and perhaps a couple of others. Once aboard we would transport them to the interrogation / prisoner of war point where they would be questioned. We wouldn't wait for the interrogation to complete we would just drop them off and rejoin the pink team. (Red bird + White bird = Pink Team)

The squads of Blues and the slicks would rotate the Hawk missions, so everyone had an equal opportunity to die. We actually rotated all of the missions so that no one crew or squad was exposed more than the other, and any mission flown would be random.

We had been doing these hawk flights all morning. I think we all had at least one or two flights apiece. We found out at lunch that we had been pretty successful in the morning. A couple of the folks who were selected and we picked up turned out to be a paymaster, and another some senior officer. We were so successful that we were sent out again that afternoon.

I was in the operations bunker—a two room above ground, no windowed sandbagged bunker—when we heard the excitement over the radio as one of the Hawk flights was being put in. The red bird had been shot down—launch the Blues! The Red Bird shot down was our troop commander, Major George Burrow. He is a singular circumstance; a man of unquestioned personal valor and a real hero, but somewhat of a magnet ass.

The Blues are a hard core platoon of infantry who are assigned directly and organic to the Air Cavalry Troop. The Blues lived with the Blue Lift section, a group of 8—10 pilots who flew the lift ships, which transported them in and out of the LZs. Also organic to the troop were 10 redbirds which are Huey gunships (B and C models), and 10 white birds (H-13s) which were little two person scout helicopters with bubbles and a tail boom resembling an erector set.

As one might imagine, these troops were a tight team, and the bonds developed were very strong. There was a belief among the 1/9 CAV Troopers that if they ever went down to be careful because the rest of the troop would have mid-airs trying to get them out.

We inserted the Blues into the hot LZ where Burrow's aircraft sat, and went after the ready reaction force, which we knew, would be standing on ramp alert, ready to assist our Blues. We picked up the reaction force intending to insert them with the Blues to reinforce them, however, while picking them up, another of our ships was shot down. We diverted and inserted the reaction force on top of the second aircraft.

The ready reaction force was committed immediately. While we were inserting them, another unit was alerted. We put that unit in also, a little while later.

As the action progressed more and more aircraft were to be shot up trying to get crews out, or while trying to secure the aircraft which had been shot down. This was one hell of afternoon. Other authors have told the battle story after reconstructing it from message logs and after battle reports. Others, I am sure, tell different versions of some particulars. I will leave them to tell the "official" story here's how I remember the day.

Suffice it to say the afternoon was quite an experience. Birds getting shot up and limping back to the safety of LZ Porazzo, our forward laager area, or getting shot down in the rice paddies. Typically the Troop's job was to go look for the enemy, establish and maintain contact with them, while we went back and brought in a company of regular infantry (a ready reaction force) who was better equipped and manned to fight the battle. One of the Blues priorities, of course, was to secure downed aircraft and rescue the crews. A platoon of some 28—30 Blues can't secure more than one bird at a time.

We went through so many units that on my last flight in, the subject of this vignette, we were picking up units who were in contact in other locations. This was really interesting. Most times either the take off or the landing was from a secure or cold area. In this case both ends of the flight were subject to intense ground fire. The flight was made even more interesting by the fact that we were down to just two blue lift ships. My x-ray (WO1 Jack Craft) and I were in Blue 37, and WO1 Tom Maehrlein and my flight school classmate WO1 Larry Brown in Blue 36.

A plea was made over the air frequencies asking any aircraft in the vicinity that were empty and able to help in the assault to marry up with us. A number did and they fell in behind us. Blue 36 was in the lead, I flew his wing. We had no idea, except from the callsigns, who else was in the flight. They were not from the CAV.

Because of this, I am sure they will have a story to tell. The CAV does things a bit different. And this afternoon, and this situation demanded that we be really different. Because of the intense fire from the entire area there was no clear way to shoot a normal approach without getting blown out of the sky. With just a scout bird to cover the flight in we let down to tree top level and below for the final approach in. We came in screaming over the rice paddies and between the tree lines. We wanted to minimize the time any of the bad guys could see us and shoot at us.

The radios were busy as the guns and the scouts worked on top of the blues and the reaction force at the different sites. The scout bird gave us directions into the LZ. As we got real close he said " . . . when you come to the end of the left tree line take a hard left and land. That's the LZ."

" Be careful of the downed bird in the LZ," he said as an afterthought.

We were hugging the terrain at above 90 knots on this approach. As we made the turn at the end of the tree line I saw 36 honk the aircraft back to slow down. (I.e. rapidly point the nose of the aircraft up in a flare attitude to bleed off airspeed.) I did the same, standing my Huey on its tail. I had to peddle turn the tail a little to keep it out of the rice paddy. Once the forward momentum stopped I began to level the bird before it crashed tail first into the paddy. I leveled the bird, pulled in power and set the bird down quickly Even before touching down Dunn was yelling at the troops to get off the aircraft.

I am sure the guys flying the aircraft behind us had a difficult job at it too, though I sensed they hung back a bit from us. Since these weren't our Blues, who ride the skids in and jump off between 3 and 5 feet above the ground, we had to actually land in the LZ. The crew chief was yelling at the troops to speed their departure. (Actually he was yelling "get the f*ck off! Move out!) Three-six was first in, so naturally he was first out. I watched as I waited for these grunts to offload, as 36 climbed straight out of the LZ. As he gained altitude I could see streams of tracers coming at him from what appeared to be from all sides. Over the radio Wonder Warthog chided me, "37 you're gonna get shot at" in a childlike neener-neener-neener tone. Seeing that and hearing Wonder I said to myself "you went out high and got shot at, I'll go out low. Watch this shit Wonder . . ."

The crew chief yelled, "we're up!" over the intercom. Finally, I thought to myself as I scanned the gauges to make sure everything was green. Jack gave me a thumbs up as I was pulling pitch. I lifted off quickly and I popped up over the tree line and began to pick up some speed. I wanted out of there. I saw some tracers ahead so I banked sharply left when I caught a glimpse of it. A soldier in NVA garb, with his weapon pointed right my way. The next thing I know is a loud rat a tat tat, and metal ripping noise, and I can't see, and there is wind and stuff in my face. The back of neck felt red-hot. I said "I'm hit, you got it" to my x-ray. Jack Craft, my co-pilot came back with "I've got the controls." And I released my grip and tried to figure out what went wrong and what the condition of the aircraft was. I wiped my eyes and face and it hurt.

I begin to take an inventory. I had trouble focusing my eyes but I could still see a little. My face was scraped and peppered with Plexiglas that came from the windscreen shattered by some of the rounds that hit us. In microseconds I felt us climbing. Jack, my new guy x-ray, was climbing! "No we'll get killed up there" I told myself. Then I said, "I've got the controls" and got us back screaming on the trees.

I looked at the master caution light and the segmented lights. Though I couldn't focus on them, it looked like they all were on. I looked at the engine instruments, again not able to focus. It looked like the needles were out of range. We had rotated the round dials of the engine instruments so that when the instruments were reading in the normal range the needles or pointers were all pointing towards the nine o'clock position. Now it looked like each was in a different time zone. I asked the crew chief, Dunn, what did it look like—I can't read the gauges. Dunn said "It looks bad Mr. F, it looks really bad. You better put her down before she comes apart." I told Dunn to point me to an open area. Dunn directed me by saying "come left, a little more, now straight, right in front of you. Put her down."

I began to flare for the landing. Somewhere during this time I called Wonder on the radio and said "36, this is 37, I'm going down." Wonder Warthog came back with a dry almost I told you so, "Roger, out."

"Nice guy" I thought. No, 'roger I'm on the way back for you' or anything; just "roger, out." I didn't have time to dwell on it, however, I was pretty busy.

Dunn was firing his M60 machine gun at the tree line on the left of the LZ as I shot the approach. A one gun prepping of the LZ. I was puzzled, I would here the M-60's rat-tat-ta-tat-ta-tat-ta-tat-Stop. Rat-a-tat-ta-tat-ta-tat-ta-tat-Stop. Rat tat-ta-tat-ta-tat-tat-Stop. I couldn't understand the stopping. Each time I knew the gun had jammed, but no, momentarily the gun would again fire. I swung around to look and I could see the cause. What I saw was funny, really funny. You see the gun stopped firing because Dunn wore glasses that rode down his nose from the vibrations of the gun firing. You would here rat-tat-ta-tat-ta-tat-ta-tat-Stop. Rat-a-tat-ta-tat-ta-tat-ta-tat-Stop. Rat tat-ta-tat-ta-tat-tat-Stop. The stop was where he would momentarily stop firing and push the glasses back up on his nose.

The prep must have worked, because we didn't get any more hits into us. The engine stayed with us until the very end. We touched down quickly, and rocked forward just a bit. Not too hard, but we were definitely down. At some point in the final seconds of the "approach" I thought I heard someone say over the radio "I'm following him in." I wasn't really conscious of it though.

We touched down in the wet, muddy rice paddy. We shut the aircraft down. Fuel Off. Throttle closed. Battery switch off. Dunn jumped out, still with his M60, and an arm full of linked ammo, and popped open my door, and slide my armor plating back so I could get out. I tried to get out but had to come back in and unfasten my seatbelt. I slipped on the skid and landed in the wet paddy. Dunn almost picked me up with one arm and began pushing me around the front of the helicopter.

In fact, one of the birds that joined up with us for the assault had indeed followed me in and was waiting in the paddy about 15 meters away. I could see Jack Craft ahead of us running low towards the awaiting bird. Dunn and I came around the front of our bird and I hesitated on the right side of the nose. There in the rice paddy was the co-pilot's door laying flat in the paddy. I was confused as to how it got there? The touchdown wasn't that hard. "Never mind that now" I said to myself as Dunn and I made it to the bird and crawled aboard. As soon as we were in, the bird lifted off, enroute to the LZ Baldy and the medical aid station.

During the lift off I quickly checked the crew asking "if everything was okay" with each of them.

Dunn said "Yep, I'm good."

Jack said "Yeah, I'm fine."

Then he added, "Ya'know? I'm glad we got shot down today."

I almost killed him; what the hell was he talking about? He continued, "All through flight school you sit in the seat and see that big yellow and black T-handle safety wired down with the words "Emergency Use Only". Today I got my chance to see how it worked!"

That's why the door was off the aircraft and laying in the rice paddy—Jack had pulled the emergency handle. I'm glad I made Jack's day for him. Once we were clear of the site and enroute to LZ Baldy I thanked the crew enthusiastically—I was some lucky guy. This was the first time I had ever been hit—-almost eight months with the Troop—-, though not a record, something unusual.

I had left the aircraft in a bit of a hurry. And as we were told over and over again in training, "if it ain't strapped on you, it ain't gonna get out in a crash." I learned the lesson again. Pilots were issued either 38 or 45 caliber pistols as their weapon. Most of us however also drew an additional weapon. I drew a neat XM-128 (I think that was the correct nomenclature or name of the weapon.) It had a three round magazine of 40mm grenades. A super chunker, if you will. Well I didn't have it strapped to me so it remained in the aircraft. Also in the aircraft I left my acetate covered tactical map, with all the firebases, and LZs pictured on it. And I left my Aussie style bush hat with its Blue band and the 1st9th Brass on it under my seat. Some body got a couple of real good souvenirs that afternoon.

Since we always carried the same squad of Blues on board, I also carried extra stuff for them. These included cigarettes, candy, and sometimes, other stuff. This day, I had a mostly filled case of C-4 (composition 4) explosives in front of the transmission wall. We were lucky nothing had hit that during our unexpected landing.

We were very lucky that day indeed. Within about ten minutes of our touchdown the dinks had gotten to the aircraft, ripped off my chunker, my map and most of the C-4. The remainder of the C-4 they used to blow up the aircraft.

"Baby Snooks," named for that girl in Howard Beach, my brand new H model Huey, which I got shortly after being made an aircraft commander, was destroyed. But my crew and I made it out okay. Thanks to the Lord, and to that crew whoever they are, who came in to get us.

They dropped us at the aid station at LZ Baldy. The doctors flushed my eyes and washed most of the plexiglass from my face. They said I should be careful shaving because the plexiglass would probably be working its way out of the skin for a while. After being cleared by the medics we hopped a flight back to Chu Lai, where together with the rest of the aircrews who had been shot up and down that day, we went to the club and got ripped! We toasted our Troop Commander, Major George Burrow, who as we spoke, was in the rice paddy with our Blues spending one of their rare overnights out in the field.

The next day written on the operations briefing map in the Troop CP, CPT Bert Chole, our operations officer had lettered " 13 November, a Day to Remember."

Shortly after the 13th General Tolson flew in and presented a lot of medals to our guys. I received my second award of the Distinguished Flying Cross, and Jack got his first. Tolson also paid his respects and spoke of the heroism of our comrades who died or were wounded.

A few years ago Bert began calling a few of us each November 13th to say hello. I ran into Bert a number of times over my career in the Army. After I retired I ran into Bert again working on the same project and the same company, and we have remained in touch. Thanks to the Vietnam Helicopter Pilots Association Bert and I and many of the folks mentioned in this manuscript meet once a year on the 4th of July.

When we finally pulled the Blues out and got them home the next day, there were a lot of stories being told. One was of Major Burrow staying out with them overnight. They reported that he had his trusty 38 caliber out as he went from dike to dike checking on the troops and the situation there, and ensuring the Blues were alert.

At the LZ Porazzo OPs bunker a few days later, MAJ Burrow was talking about that night and said he hadn't even fired his weapon that night. He wondered aloud, "Hell I wonder if it even shoots." With that he went to the test fire pit at the perimeter, drew his pistol and pulled the trigger. Nothing. The gun was jammed and wouldn't fire. Of course, no one can say whether the gun was working the night in the paddy, and the time since that night had caused the pistol to malfunction, or whether the pistol was unable to fire that night!

Earlier in the week Mike Covey and I were flying together and doing Hawk Flights. On one of them Larry had spotted a lot of military aged males working in a rice field and sent us in as the Red Bird provided cover overhead.

I set up a pattern for the approach to the rice paddy. The paddy looked like a busy place with lots of folks peacefully working together. As I turned on to final approach, something didn't look right. I realized what was wrong as the squad of Blues exited the aircraft at their normal 3-5 feet. The rice paddy had become rather sparse of people. I set down in the paddy as we usually do and wait for the Blues to just grab a few folks and then we leave. Well this was to be different.

The field lay alongside a river that defined the right and rear sides of the LZ where we landed. The other two sides were composed of two tree lines with the village tucked behind the tree lines. We were about 100 or 150 meters away from the tree line.

The Blues went running in different directions trying to catch some of the remaining males. All of a sudden and out of nowhere all hell broke loose. The left tree line opened fire on us. The Blues instantaneously returned fire. I grabbed for a bunch of collective pitch to get the bird out of there. Mike held the collective down saying we can't leave the Blues here. He was right. We couldn't leave the Blues there.

I yelled into the fox mike radio to the squad leader to get back on board. I wasn't getting any response at all. I looked at the RTO (radio man) and found out why no one was responding—the handset to the microphone was dangling at the side of his pants as he and the other Blues stood there in the paddy and peppered the tree line with automatic fire. Larry was working the tree line as well. Strafing it with his skid gun and his observer's M60.

Here we were stuck in the middle of an LZ in the middle of a firefight. Flanagan I told myself, this is the day you've known was coming. For the first time since arriving in Vietnam my crew chief was working out on his M60 machine gun.

Rounds were kicking up all around us in the paddy. They were hitting right in front of my chin bubble—spattering mud and dirty rice paddy water over the windscreen. I knew I had to get the hell out of there. I picked the Huey to a hover and hovered back and over to each of the Blues so they could get on and we could get out of there. Larry and the gun bird had put enough stuff on the tree line to keep their heads down. We were able to get the Blues on and got out of there, pronto.

The Blues even brought along one of the guys working in the rice paddy. This guy turned out to be an officer in the NVA we would come to find out weeks later.

I called operations on the way back to drop the prisoner off. Burrow asked me how we were doing. I told we were all right I think. He asked if we needed anything. I told him no, but make us reservations at the shitter when we get back I had to clean out my pants. He rogered the transmission and we all had a good laugh. I am sure glad Mike was with me that day; he was right we couldn't leave the Blues in the LZ.

Our Chaplains Were Different Life in B Troop, 1/9 CAV during my time in 1967 to 1968 was a strange mix of realities. I don't know how to explain them but life was definitely different. Even after talking with pilots from other units, who units admittedly did some strange things, I can safely say B 1/9 was different and unique.

"How different," you ask? Even our chaplains were different. To demonstrate the point here are two examples:

After one very hot and exciting day in the midst of many consecutively exciting days at LZ Porazzo, we retired to the club. It had been a really bad day. A number had been shot down and we had lost a couple of folks. God forgive me, I don't remember their names. In any case, we went to the club. As was customary the Old Man and sometimes the chaplain would come to the club with us. As was also customary the Ol'man would leave early so we could really get into forgetting. This one night as the Old Man was leaving he stood up, turned to the chaplain and asked "You coming with me, Chaplain?'

Our Chaplain replied quickly, " No sir, it's not everyday a Chaplain gets a chance to lead his flock astray!"

If you believe that was what the Chaplain was doing I've got a bridge to sell you in my hometown. That chaplain stayed there and took care us, as we went about our business of forgetting. I can almost recall him with us descending from the club on the hill, arms about each other's shoulders as this chorus line of 6 or 8 B Troopers sang and staggered our way back to the hooches.

I vividly recall one time while coming down the hill where we stopped momentarily, mid-stride and mid-chorus, while one in our number leaned forward and with a force equal to that of the pressure of a 2 1/2 inch fire hose, evacuated his stomach contents. And then within a couple of seconds, we picked up the step and the chorus and proceeded on, laughing a bit louder and deeper.

Instrument Approach Another time I was flying with Jack Craft as my x-ray with the Chaplain aboard going into Qui Nhon. On this leg we were coming in from Duc Pho to Qui Nhon, and the weather was forecast to be not VFR (visual flight rules). Jack and I both had been trained in instruments and given an Army

Tactical Instrument ticket. These were little more than licenses to kill us. But as 20 year old pilots, we feared nothing. Of course we weren't dumb either. The Chaplain was a prior marine aviator, who had a lot of experience flying instruments—in fighters, not helicopters. But what the hell! I figured if he could talk on the radio, and tune the beacons I could fly the course.

Arriving over Qui Nhon there was an undercast between the ground and us. We had enough fuel to get down, but not enough to really do anything else. The chaplain talked on the radio, and I flew the approach. Luckily the approach was a GCA so as soon as we got lined up the radar operator talked us down. The weather didn't require an approach to the minimums but it did require an instrument approach in the clouds. This was the first time I had ever been in the clouds and shot an approach for real.

Where else, I ask you, do you find chaplains that aren't afraid of the congregation getting a bit shit faced, or helping a pilot get below the clouds.

Thanks, Chaplains wherever you are.

* There are tales from our red platoon of one of our chaplains riding as a door gunner with them, and being quite a good marksman at that. I am sure it is true, but I can't say I saw it myself.

Serving the Troops I would be remiss if I didn't acknowledge the very moving, solemn and inspiring services they conducted for us in remembrance of our fallen comrades. Our Chaplains knew us, and knew many of the young men we were remembering. There were a number of men who we didn't really know, they being killed very shortly after joining us. Our chaplains were always able to say from their hearts just the right things.

They helped again in a very stressful situation. At Two Bits one of our squads was accused of gang raping a village women one night while they were on patrol. The squad might have gotten off except for one of the members turning government witness in return for the charges being dropped. The guys in the squad were great guys. Decent, young Americans they really were. Unfortunately they were in a terrible place seeing terrible things every day. And they made a mistake, a big mistake, and they paid a big, very big price. They and their families back home had to pay a very big price for that mistake and lapse in judgement.

The squad was sent back to An Khe and restricted to a separate barracks in the troop area. I visited with them a couple of times while they were awaiting their courts-martial. I felt and still feel sorry for what happened to them. And I still feel anger for the guy who turned on them. I also feel bad for the woman and her family. But it is Smitty's squad and their families that I feel for the most. I didn't think the sentences were fair back then, and I still don't think them fair today. Although I know what they did was wrong, and I know they deserved to be punished. I still can't accept it as being fair.

The squad was found guilty and sent to the Disciplinary Barracks at Fort Leavenworth, Kansas. I don't know how long they had to spend there, but I think of them often, and remember them with prayer.

I think our Chaplain helped the guys with prayer and individual counseling.

Chicken Fights We had a lot of fun at Chu Lai. We were living good. The housing was the best we ever had. Working out of the forward LZ was super. The base was so big that I don't even think we had anybody have to pull perimeter guard as we had to everyplace else.

We worked hard in the daytime, and played hard at night.

At night after chow we would mosey up the hilltop the club and just relax. We would sing, tell stories, and joke around. Just have a ball, and try to relax. I don't know what time the club closed, really. It probably closed at 9 or 10 PM or so. One night we were there and closed the club and were horsing around outside. We began to play chicken fights. You know the game, a guy gets on another guy's back and you try to push the other guys off their mounts. We were having a great old time laughing and playing around, when all of sudden a deep authoritative voice came out of the darkness.

It said "At ease, you better cut that out and get to your areas."

Don Burnham who I don't recall whose back he was on says back "You better be more than a senior O-3 (Captain) to say that."

The voice came back: "Will an O5 (Lieutenant Colonel) do?"

"Yes sir," we said almost together, and headed quickly down the hill.

Opposite Faces Of War The Chu Lai Officer's Club was a contrast in the realities of war. Here came together the combat pilots from the toughest Air Cavalry Squadron in the history of the universe, and the meekest staff pukes that any division ever had. (I'll try not to hold back anymore.) Actually there were probably some absolute heroes on that staff, but they didn't make up for some of the pukes that we ran into at the club.

The mix of men in the club was an absolute contrast in personalities, missions, and priorities, with the commonality of trying to get through the days until we could each go home. Here were the pilots who have just cheated death for the umpteenth time blowing off some steam. Loud and boisterous sometime. Perhaps even to excess, a time or two. And drinking a lot trying to calm down from the day, and preparing ourselves for the next day. Also in the club were staff officers who probably had an equally troublesome day. I overheard one guy complain to a table mate for about tem minutes the problems he was having keeping his typewriters in an operational condition, and about having to do so many OER over because the typewriters would screw up. (Officer Efficiency Reports were very important and they needed to be perfect.) They looked down on us because we were not acting

Photo Courtesy of Jim Pratt

Jim and I became "aces" that day. We downed five jet helicopters in a few short seconds. Unfortunately, they were ours.
The damage to ours is obvious by the photo. As we were crashing
our main rotor system went down the line end over end and got
two gunships; the tail rotor and some other flying parts did some
minor damage to two other aircraft when they came down. The
transmission landed at the head of the revetment. We were very
lucky that no one was hurt.

The accident investigation officer from squadron came in
and swore we had put our tail rotor into the dirt and that caused
the accident. About five days later, the Blues while policing up
the perimeter found the missing "red" tail rotor blade. When
maintenance inspected it with the accident investigators they
found the cause of the crash was from the tail rotor blade separation due to a fatigue crack.

Jim has never forgiven me for destroying his ship that day.

properly in Officers' Club; and we didn't think much of them because of their non-role in prosecuting the war.

The contrast of cultures was always evident, every so often erupting in some words or a few thrown punches. Back in those days rank did not exist in the clubs and it wasn't a career killer to have a loud disagreement with a senior. Today it is almost career ending just to be seen in a club more a few times during an assignment.

There were a number of close calls, but no lasting fights occurred. This I am sure is because our commissioned leaders looked after us on the ground.

On the bright side, we also had Vietnamese waitresses at the club. Though they spoke just a little English, they quickly learned how to communicate in English some of the most important concepts of the time. That is, getting a drink order straight for a bunch of thirsty Air Cavalrymen. The girls learned how to say scotch and water, or bourbon and water, or Budweiser pretty quickly. However the complexities of the mixology sometimes challenged them. Ordering a "scotch on the rocks" was one of these challenges. They soon learned to overcome the challenge by ordering the bartender to make a "scotch and water—no water."

One evening a couple of our guys were sitting listening to somebody else talking about how tough a guy was in their unit. They said this guy would break glasses on his forehead. The time grew late, and the beer and liquor flowed easily, and sometimes I guess, a WO maintenance officer just gets fed up and has to do something. Good old Clark picks up his empty high ball glass and crushes it into his forehead, and continues to drink his other drink. Bleeding a lot he left shortly after finishing his drink and got some 13 or so stitches in his head. Someone quoted him years later as saying "breaking glasses is easy, crushing them is the tough part."

Overlooking LZ Ross—Late November or early December 1967 Larry Brown, Grif Bedworth, Terry Connor, Dave Bressam and I joined B Troop 1/9 Cavalry in early April 1967. By the time, we moved up to Chu Lai only Larry and I remained in country.

Grif was killed as a result of a weather accident while returning to An Khe to receive his commission to Lieutenant. Terry had taken a few rounds in the thigh (maybe buttocks, too) while flying guns with the troop commander, MAJ Beasley. Dave Bressam was evac'd to the states after having a gunship explode while he and the Blues were trying to rescue the crew. Dave had gone out on the ground with the Blues on his day off.

Larry and I formed quite a bond when it came down to us and we had a long time to go, and much to be done, before we could go home. We knew that together we would either go home, or not. When Larry was out in his white bird I would stay in OPs waiting to be the first one to him if anything happened; likewise Larry would stand by when I was out, just in case I needed some cover. The back up was unofficial, but it worked.

Launch the Blues! Larry had come across and killed a small party of folks on a hilltop overlooking LZ Ross at the mouth of the Que Son valley. We put the Blues in and orbited while they checked the bodies. Some firing occurred while the Blues were on the ground. Later we learned a paymaster was hiding under another body and had tried to fire at one of the bodies from behind. Another Blue noticed him and got him first.

As the reports came in from the Blues the situation became more interesting. This wasn't just any small tactical unit. These guys were senior NVA officers, wearing pistols. The blues recovered the weapons. They also reported finding intelligence papers. Then a call came that woke me up. They reported finding a "map. Just like the ones the pilots' use."

Could it be? Could this be my map? The one that was captured on 13 November, the day I got shot down?

I called the Blues and said for them to give the map to the

squad riding my aircraft back. We made the pickup from the LZ and, once airborne, they passed up an acetate tactical map, just like mine. In fact it proved to be mine! Under the acetate was hand written: " WO1 John Flanagan, The CAV Sucks!" That was mine all right. The only differences were, there were all kinds of arrows and diagrams—battle plans—drawn on it showing a planned attack on LZ Ross, and of course, there was the blood and stuff from the guy who had been holding my map. This incident has been written about in a lot of books. In at least one of these books finding the map with the enemy plans was credited with preventing LZ Ross from being overrun.

When we dropped off the map and papers confiscated at the Compound I asked that my map be returned. They didn't return it. But at least we got even for losing "Baby Snooks."

I still get ribbed about my map. Not for leaving it in the aircraft, or even for Larry finding it again, but rather because when they checked my map they found out that I had plotted almost every one of the LZs in the wrong place. They weren't too far off but they were plotted differently. Perhaps that's way the NVA Generals were on the hilltop, trying to see if the LZ had moved to the position I had on my map. My reasoning for the misplots were that, hell, if I get that close to the firebase or LZ I'll be able to see the damn thing. Who cares about plotting accuracy.

The Square Lake The lift platoon worked mainly as a flight reacting to the tactical situation. Most times I had no real idea of where we were going exactly. Just that we were going to insert the Blues at such and such set of coordinates. We didn't even use coordinates we used a technique of shifting from a known point. So for example a name was given to each intersection of the 22 and 42 grid lines. If the name given was Bacon, then something 2500 meters to the right of that point, and 1000 meters south of that point would be sent over the air as "from Bacon right 2.5, drop 1.0." Since the bad guys didn't know which intersection we were using, or the name given to each intersection, we fooled ourselves into believing that we were secure.

The scouts and the guns were different. They were always all over the map. They became quite familiar with the terrain and the entire area of operations. They even began naming things. The twin humps, for an area in the foothills that had a nice pair of hilltops.

One day at Porazzo, I was playing hearts when the call came to launch 37 and contact 6 in the air. We all ran to the aircraft. The crewchief untied and swung the rotor blade 90 degrees, grabbed the fire extinguisher and responded with "clear," as I called to "clear" just prior to cranking the engine. The Blues were in the last stages of mounting the aircraft as the engine came to full operating RPM and I lifted off. On liftoff I contacted 6 and asked told him I was airborne. He said " 37 rendezvous with me over the square lake." Square lake? Where the hell is the square lake? Quickly I grabbed the map and began to frantically search for a square lake. I found one to the southeast. As I came over the square lake I reported in to 6. "6, 37, I'm over the square lake at 500feet."

He responded that he didn't see me. I told him I didn't see him either. After a few tense filled minutes I had to admit I was over the wrong square lake. 6 told me that his square lake was northwest of Porazzo. Off we went. I took a heading off Porazzo and found another square lake. Reporting in to Six again I said, "6, 37, I'm now over the second square lake." 6 said he didn't see me. I told him, I didn't see him either. After about 30 minutes of this stuff 6 canceled the mission, he had to refuel.

I constantly got ribbed over this square lake, but no one has ever been able to show me on the map where this damn square lake was.

I was reminded of this square lake fiasco while visiting Fort Hood Texas a few weeks ago. I was observing a battalion task force performing training for their upcoming rotation to the National Training Center. They were using a brand new set of simulators, which replicated each crews' combat vehicle. They were all networked together moving around in a virtual reality replication of the NTC. Over the radio and throughout the conversations the leaders were talking about the "peanut" and the "race track," etc. During the after action review of the battle it became clear that not everyone in the unit understood clearly where these named places were, exactly. The senior trainer recommended highly that instead of using these nicknames, they should rely on the good old military grid designations.

I was prepared to stand up and fess up to the "square lake" episode, but it appeared they understood the lesson without a confession.

Duck wall Every morning at Chu Lai we would saddle up the Blues and launch at first light enroute to LZ Porazzo. We would lift off the Saber Pad and follow the road out to the perimeter trying to avoid overflying the American Division's Headquarters. We would turn north and flying low level pass over the large expanse of lake that bordered the base to the north. Flying north at a low level became a time to relax and a time for fun.

The Blues would be catching their last few winks of sleep, or be going through the last stages of the wake up process. We would fly a loose formation.

An otherwise peaceful time of the morning with the sun rising from the sea to the east we would head north. The farmers would be getting going just as millions of other people do around the world start their day with a healthy constitutional. Here in Vietnam eliminating body waste was a bit more visible. There were no bathrooms in the villages. They did it out in the open by squatting over the field from a rice paddy dike. I guess it made sense. Why not use your own fertilizer in your own fields? In the morning you could see the farmers squatted down on the dikes. Occasionally we would break from the formation and set up a low level run at the farmers. Depending on which way the old guy was looking approach him differently. The best was when he was facing you. You line up on him and keep getting lower and lower until it looks like your skids are on the same level with his head. Then you play chicken. Now if their backs was turned away then you needed to approach at an angle so you can see their faces when they finally realized you're about to hit them.

It really is funny to see them. Either they would try to finish what they are doing and get out of there, or, as was the case for many, to jump into the paddy to avoid getting hit. In retrospect we may have even helped them evacuate themselves better than Ex-Lax. Sometimes we got pretty close to them. There are some stories going around about a scout pilot coming in with a straw hat attached to the front of one of the skids.

On one particular morning we took off and were clicking along over the lake on an exceptionally beautiful morning. The lake was like polished glass, smooth and clear, reflecting the images of our aircraft as pictures of its surface.

There is nothing like being in the air in the morning. The world is so fresh, and the day so young, it must color the mind because I have so many beautiful scenes in the morning. This day was one of the more beautiful and peaceful. A flight of four Hueys, low over the water at sunrise, in a tight little formation without a care in the world. It must have been a beautiful sight. From my cockpit a beautiful day had begun.

Then. Instantly! A wall of ducks appeared directly in front of us. They must have been roosting there over night, and the suddenness of our approach and noise from our aircraft must have spooked them. They were everywhere! From the surface up to 300 feet or so. And we were right in the middle of them, and could do nothing to avoid or react to them. All that I know is that thew sky was clear; then there were ducks. And then there were the loud noises of the ducks hitting the aircraft And then there were the sounds of the awakening Blues charging their weapons, and releasing the safeties on their weapons preparing to return fire. And then there were more birds impacting the airframe and windscreen. I did see one duck flaring frantically in front of the right side windscreen, and flapping his wings to beat all hell trying to avoid us. He had his feet down so that he may be able to land on us. The closer he came to the windscreen the faster the wings flapped. No go. He smacked right into the upper right part of the windscreen splattering blood and feathers through Jack's open side window and into the aircraft. It even splattered some blood and guts onto the Blue sitting on the jumpseat in back of Jack.

Man the situation was wild! There was no place to go to avoid these things and the Blue Flight formation just held together. Wonder took a duck through the chin bubble. I took another duck on my aft pylon just missing my tail rotor. Every aircraft took hits that morning. The radio was lit up with chatter as this happened. Once we knew everyone was okay, we began describing the damage and the experience to each other. When we got to Porazzo we went from aircraft to aircraft inspecting the shot pattern, and laughing like hell. Everyone had a story to tell. The guns and scouts came over to inspect the damage and laugh with us.

The Blues who were rudely awakened by the mid-airs tell some of the best accounts of the incident. The Blues thought we had been hit by some of those 37 mm anti aircraft guns. Thankfully no one got really hurt.

WO Bill Beaverslus was our liaison to the Brigade at LZ Baldy that day. He coordinated with the 3rd Brigade Headquarters operations each day ensuring that the ground troops knew where we were operating and coordinated the ready reaction force of straight leg grunts when once our Blues had made contact with the enemy.

He monitored the radio discussions and promptly posted on the Brigade Activity Board that B Troop had destroyed thirteen B1-RDs. Many of the folks in the brigade tactical operations center stopped by to ask the Beav what type weapon system a B1-RD was. The Beav enjoyed pulling a couple of legs that day.

I guess after this day we were never as complacent flying over the lake in the morning again.

Chapter Thirteen

Good-bye Americal—Hello Camp Evans

All good things must come to an end. And our time at Chu Lai had certainly come to an end. We had trained the new CAV unit that just came in from the States. Blue Ghost, the 7/17 CAV was to be Americal's reconnaissance squadron. Many of the pilots were flight school classmates of mine and I enjoyed seeing them again. Seeing them was especially good, because we were halfway through our tour, while they had just begun theirs. It felt good to be short, I remember. Almost like being in your senior year and you just realize that you have taken all but your final exam.

We were given the word that we were to move further north to Camp Evans. Camp Evans was about halfway between the City of Hue, and Quang Tre. Quang Tre was just south of the DMZ, the line separating South from North Vietnam. Camp Evans was a relatively small, quiet firebase. Things were about to change as the 1ˢᵗ of the 9ᵗʰ moved northward again. We didn't know it at the time, but the squadron headquarters was coming up with us, and our Charlie Troop was going up to Quang Tre.

On the day of the move we began ferrying our equipment and personal stuff from Chu Lai up to Evans. First we carried the tents, and then we started carrying gear and supplies. Finally we carried our personal stuff. We also slung load the shitters we had up, to Evans. On the last lift out, despite repeated orders from the Americal Division Commander and his staff not to overfly his headquarters, we did. Every single aircraft we had, flew over his headquarters. A few more enterprising souls "accidentally" dropped a couple of CS grenades on the Division headquarters as they went over. (CS Gas is a very heavy tear gas agent used to get dinks out of bunkers and spider holes.)

I understand that Major Burrow received a royal ass chewing for this, but we never heard anything more about it; he never passed it on down the line. I think he sort of enjoyed the thought of gassing the Headquarters.

Arriving at Evans they put us outside of the perimeter. We had to set up outside of the wire. We were to live there in bad guy land until we could construct a new perimeter. We set up the tents and then tried to figure out what the quickest way was to get some safety from grazing fire or incoming mortar rounds. We didn't have enough time, or energy for that matter, to fill enough sandbags to sandbag the tent. Instead, we each set about seeking a personal solution. What I did was dig three, eight inch or so deep trenches that the legs of my cot fit down into. Thus the bottom of my cot was just a few inches from the ground. Then I filled enough sandbags to place off to the side of the bunk so that I had a place to roll into. My area was not very comfortable, or very safe I am sure. But it served its purpose I was able to get some sleep that night. I remember waking up throughout the night thinking that I heard someone coming too close. And also waking with the horrible thought that there was a snake inside my mosquito netting.

I've never liked snakes. Whenever I thought about the possibility of a snake getting into my bunk or my boots, I would have to convince myself or talk myself into believing there were no snakes in my area. I knew I was playing a mind game, but it worked.

A few days after we arrived at Camp Evans, an engineer lieutenant came to the troop area to see what support his guys could give us. As it turned out the lieutenant and I had been in the same platoon during basic training. Duke was his name. He was as surprised to see me as a pilot as I was to see him as a lieutenant. Duke was okay, he gave us a bulldozer operator who cut parking slots into the slope for the Blue Platoon helicopters. This reduced the number sandbags we had to fill to complete the revetment.

The days were filled with a lot of activity as we made yet another place our home. We were fortunate to have the sea so close. Instead of us having to fill all the sand bags, Top would send a truck and some money out each morning and they would hire some locals to fill sand bags for us. If I recall correctly it cost us about two piasters a sand bag, with a piaster worth about 1/3 of a cent.

The nights were something else. The artillery unit was right next to us, just inside the wire. When the artillery would fire over our tents the concussion would lift you off your air mattress. (And my wife can't understand how I can sleep with the TV on all night.)

A few days after arriving we had to relocate the tent. We were in monsoon season now—rainy and surprisingly cold. Somewhere during the move we had lost the exhaust pipes (chimney pipes) for our tent stoves. Wonder Warthog and Covey came up with the idea of using the shipping tubes that the artillery rounds came in. They were about the right diameter and length. They fashioned the tubes into exhaust pipes and lit fires in the stoves. We were working outside the tents, filling sand bags for the revetments, or some such thing when we looked up to see flames and heavy black smoke shooting out the top of the tubes. Man what a fire! Luckily, we were able to get the tubes down and out of the tent before it caught the whole tent on fire, and luckily no one was burned either. We did suffer a lot of little pinholes in the top of the tent the result of burning embers. Of course, they were never important enough to try to fix unless rain was beating on the tent like hell and the roof was leaking over your bunk. Then we all would be out in the rain trying to mend the tent.

Just setting up like we did, the supply lines hadn't caught up with us. At one point we were eating C-rations everyday. We didn't have any hot rations—i.e. real food—for what seemed to be a week. We had heard that the Squadron Headquarters unit that moved up after us had begun to get real meals. George said we were going to have fresh meat tomorrow. He didn't quite explain what he meant. That afternoon, Larry Brown went out and shot a wild water buffalo, and one of the guys slung load the animal back under a Huey. The mess sergeant and a couple of cooks skinned and butchered the buffalo out in back of the mess tent.

The next morning bleary eyed, cold and drearily we moved through the chow line. Today the cooks were serving up steak and scrambled eggs for breakfast. I had told myself it's gonna be all right until I glanced in the back of the mess tent where I saw a hoof sticking out of one of the big cooking pots. I ate the water buffalo steak and found it much better than having C rations again. I don't know what happened after that really. I don't know how squadron found out, or what was said between George and the squadron. But I do know we had real meat from then on in.

At Evans we got serious about the bad guys, and the need for bunkers. Evans hadn't been hit for months before we arrived. Within a couple of days of our arrival, however, incoming rockets and mortars were common every other night or so.

Tom and Mike dug a tremendous hole in the ground. Actually about 1/8 of an inch deeper than Tom's height. It didn't matter that Mike was five inches taller than Tom, and would have to stoop to get in, Tom stopped digging when he could stand up, and that's how deep it was to be. Across the top of the bunker they had put some scrounged up PSP plating and covered the top with a lot of sandbags. So many bags were on top of the bunker there was some serious conversation and betting among the rest of us that the sheer weight of the sandbags and metal would be enough to collapse the roof.

The rest of us just dug little trenches next to the cots. I understand that when Tom and Mike got ready to leave the Troop to DEROS (Date Estimated to Return from Overseas—i.e. the day they were to go home) they sold it to Jack Craft and LT Walls for $100. A couple of days after Tom and Mike left, the Troop was ordered to move south.

I was getting short by this time. Probably getting to be a ninety-day loss. I had been there long enough that in addition to the daily ration of two cans of beer a night, I could buy more from the supply tent. I always had a case of beer under my cot.

The weather was shitty. The sky was overcast and cold and rainy. We were damp all the time. We went many days without seeing the sun. To keep warm we burned sticks of C-4 explosives. C-4 is a composite explosive that comes packaged in about 3 inch by 12 inch package. What was weird about C-4 is that it would just burn nicely and not explode unless you compressed it rapidly by stomping on it or of course using a blasting cap. We found that if you stand the sticks up on end place them in a three inch deep hole they would burn pretty evenly and give off the best heat. We burned a lot of C-4 to get warm. The fumes given off while burning smelled pretty badly, and were probably not very healthy, but at least we were warm.

Evans was a bad area. Being so close to the DMZ meant the NVA could easily mass and infiltrate the area quickly. There were a lot of intelligence reports of North Vietnam tanks being spotted in the valleys to the west, and of large units of fresh NVA troops in the mountains to the west of us.

Captain Dawson (Don) Burnham Stand. Salute. Bow in prayer. Captain Don Burnham was our platoon leader when I arrived at Duc Pho. He was a great guy. He led us into and out of more stuff than you can shake a stick at. He was always the gentleman, and the leader. It didn't matter how badly you screwed up, he dealt with it in the right way. He was always fair, and a fun guy to be around. Don was a senior captain. He was also an experienced pilot. He had been an instrument instructor at Fort Rucker before coming to Vietnam.

During our sometimes nightly songfests at the club you could hear his voice singing "swing low, sweet chariot, coming for to carry me home" in his neat southern Alabama accent. When he sang that song he appeared to be far away. I think he was back home in church with his mother in Daleville. Don was a bachelor.

Don gave up the platoon to Nubs Hirning. Nubbs was a neat guy, too. Junior to Don Burnham and it showed. But he was a good guy in his own right.

Don went and took over the aviation maintenance platoon and became our maintenance officer. Don took a flight of two aircraft on a maintenance flight to An Khe. On the way, they had planned refueling stops at Da Nang, Duc Pho, and LZ English. On the way into Da Nang the weather turned bad and the two ships split up for the instrument approaches. The second ship, piloted by WO Bill Clark landed and waited for Don. But when he didn't show up Clark contacted the controllers who said Burnham had disappeared from the radar. The controllers figured he had broken off the approach and landed visually. This was a daily occurrence when it came to army pilots, the air force controllers said. Remember most army pilots didn't have real instrument tickets, and really didn't follow all of the rules. This pilot did, however; and because of the rest of us who never reported VFR or breaking off the approach, Don and the guys on board were down for a long time before anyone went looking for them.

Da Nang is a big place and it is easy to miss someone there. The second ship reported back to operations that he and Don had split up and that he couldn't regain contact with him. Clark said he was continuing with the mission and catch up with him at An Khe.

We got word at the troop that Don was overdue and that the ramp searches turned up negative. We were all shocked! Don had been on a GCA (ground controlled approach on radar) instrument approach and they lost him on radar and they didn't appear to get excited about it. Damn. This was a second friend and ship we lost to the weather this season. First Griff and now Don Burnham crashed in weather. The troop flew down into the area and searched for days, in the hills north of Da Nang were Don had last been in contact with the controllers. Searching the hills was difficult because the weather was bad and the ceiling ragged as it lay on the ground of the valleys, draws and hills. The search was also a bit hairy, because this was a non-secure area. The bad guys were all over the place. We were lucky, no one shot at us that we knew. I don't think it would have stopped us at all, and we were certainly ready to return any hint of fire. After a few days we were called off.

Nubbs let me go out on my own a couple of times after that. I had taken the map and with the help of the transcript from the GCA, tried to trace his flight path. Again, the weather was bad and I couldn't find a trace of his aircraft. When we searched earlier we had found aircraft wreckage, but that was from previous unintended meetings with the ground.

Not until I was back at An Khe waiting to go back home did I get the news that they had found the wreckage. The wreckage was near the top of one of the hills we had searched during the bad weather. The Blues went in but all they saw was a boot and some bones, as I recall. The aircraft had burned on impact.

A lot of years later, the wife of a patient of Barry Mc Alpine's (Barry was a Blue and a squad leader during this time and was now a chiropractor in Michigan) began asking questions about the crash. Suzy had been wearing an MIA bracelet of one of the mechanics aboard Burnham's aircraft. Suzy had spent a lot of effort trying to find Joey's remains and account for the aircraft's demise. It's a small world, and nice to know there are still some people who really care.

Suzy is still on the hunt and searching for the aircraft and any remains of Joey and the others.

HUE The Imperial City of Hue was a walled city sitting along the banks of the Perfume River. Hue was the cultural center of this region. When we moved to Camp Evans I loved to overfly Hue. The colorful dresses of the women as they walked about the city were really pretty. And the walls of the City reminded me of castles of old. I really wanted to have the opportunity to go drive through that city and visit it. We had been at Evans only a short time when one morning we were told to send a team to Hue. The rest of our equipment from Chu Lai had been shipped by boat or barge, and was sitting at a dock in the Perfume River in Hue. There were reports it had been taken by the NVA. Welcome to Tet 1968.

The first light pink team headed south as soon as they took off. Arriving over the city of Hue, they reported heavy enemy activity and reported seeing an NVA flag flying from a flagpole within the Citadel. Things get a bit blurry from here on in. we were very busy, and minutes ran into days as the battle raged on. The fighting was fierce. The weather didn't cooperate either. Low ceilings, low visibility, and cold was the weather we encountered each day.

On the first or second day of action Gary Hanna, a young pilot who had been with lift up until the previous day had transferred to the guns. He was making a gun run over some troops in the vicinity of Hue when he was fatally shot. I recall that he died quickly and was not in any pain. We lost a number of folks including Gary. We had one ship shot down and the crew captured. Wonder Warthog happened over the crash site and seeing American in the center of two groups of dinks, shot an approach to the center of one group. The dinks fled, but not before they killed the two guys in the other circle of the enemy. Tom received the Distinguished Service Cross for Valor for his actions. If there was a general on the ground instead of just one of our crews, I am sure he would have certainly gotten the Medal of Honor.

During one of the early days of Tet I was at laager at a Vietnamese fire base alongside the highway just north of Hue. It became SOP to have a Blue bird and a squad of Blues there so we could react quickly to pick up any of our crews who may get shot down. PK17 was its name. The area I was in was just barely big enough for two ships. One of the scouts had had some problems with his aircraft and was able to make it almost back to PK17. He ended up parking it just outside the wire and walked in to the camp. I was sitting in the back of the Huey with a group of Blues around me shooting the bull, as Mike Covey landed beside us. Mike was coming in to relieve me, while I took the scout pilot back to Evans. I don't remember now but I think the scout pilot was either Fred Mc Murray or Jerry Elliot.

In any case Mike had no sooner set down the Huey, when a mortar round hit a short distance from my side of my aircraft spraying shrapnel all over the place. This signaled the start of a mortar attack on us. The first rounds sprayed shrapnel all over the place hitting the aircraft and some of the Blues. We automatically jumped in a nearby ditch and culvert area. I had a stream of blood trickling down the right side of my face but I didn't know from where, really. We had a couple of the Blues hit in the legs and other places. A few more rounds continued to fall. I analyzed the situation quickly and determined that since my replacement was here, and this was a gook base anyway, I was gonna take my guys and get out quickly. I yelled to my crewchief "let's go," and he and my Blues scrambled aboard. Unfortunately, I couldn't find Jack, my x-ray. I grabbed the scout pilot and told him to get in the right seat.

I cranked the aircraft as quickly as I could. As soon as the rotor came up to speed I lifted off and sped away low level to the northwest as rounds continued to fall. I climbed when I got clear of the firebase, and shouted to the scout to call the tower and get us clearance direct to the medical aid station. I looked in the back and saw one of the Blues with a pretty nasty wound to the thigh. His leg was bleeding a lot. I passed a tourniquet back to the crewchief to see if that would help. (I always carried this in my pocket in case I ever needed it.)

I looked back over to the scout who was stomping on the floor like switch trying in vain to contact the tower at Evans. I looked at him and almost rolled laughing. He hadn't plugged his helmet in yet, so all the yelling was doing no good.

I hadn't put my helmet on yet. I told you I was in a hurry. My crewchief reached up behind me and began to wipe the blood off my face near my temple. I reached up also. The wound wasn't much, just a small piece of shrapnel or something. I put my helmet on to listen to the tower. The tower advised me that a C130 was due in and that I should hold my position until he landed. Not on your life, buddy. I've got guys bleeding here, and we're coming in I told myself. I called the tower again and said, " Evans Tower, Evans Tower this is Saber Blue 37, 3 miles to the south east for direct landing to the aid station with wounded aboard. Be advised I am transmitting in the blind, I cannot understand any of your transmissions." I wasn't telling the truth of course, but it worked, and our guys didn't have to wait on some C-130 making a routine landing.

The tower called the C130 and told him to clear the pattern until he got this helicopter with radio problems on the ground. As I approached the Medevac pad there wasn't any room there for another aircraft. I continued the approach to this VIP parking area alongside one of the internal roads on Evans. I jumped out of the aircraft and went to the road where I waved over jeeps and 3/4 ton vehicles that were not loaded. We loaded the wounded Blues on them and sent them to the aid station. The crewchief sent me on the last load to check my head. The doctor said the wound was just some shrapnel that penetrated the skin. He gave me a tetanus shot, put a small bandage on it and said that I may feel some small flakes of metal every now and again. He was right. I pulled little fragments out for days. I still can feel something under the skin but it doesn't bother me enough to do anything about it.

There are too many good factual descriptions of the fight at Hue that have been written for me to try to even begin to retell it. I will tell you that I remember that the roads were cut off and our supplies lines were cut as well. With the shitty weather—low ceilings, poor visibility—they started to resupply us via low-level parachute drops outside the perimeter. I can still picture it now. I was straining to watch the bottoms of the scud layers and hearing the C130 engines getting louder and louder. And then in an instant the C130 would drop out of the scud bottom and immediately and violently nose up and "shit" pallets loaded with supplies out the back ramp of the aircraft. The parachutes attached to the pallets would just barely open before the pallets hit the ground. They hit too hard to call it a landing. Some of the chutes didn't open completely and the pallets crashed into the ground and skidded along the ground spewing the delivery all over the place. After the drops were made a unit would go out and police up the delivery. These drops went on for days at a time. This was probably the bleakest time for me.

The days of flying in shitty weather really took its toll. We were always waiting for the call to launch the Blues. The fighting was really bad. At nights the artillery battery never was quiet. The weather was cold. To use today's parlance—it sucked!

George Burrow got shot down, again at Hue. After they discovered his blind eye, he was sent home. Major Jimmy D. Weeks came in and took over as the Troop Commander. Major Weeks was an absolute gentleman, and a great leader.

I have one last remembrance of Major Burrow at Camp Evans. I was in the OPs tent with Burrow when the Squadron commander came in and started complaining about the number of aircraft we were consuming during the fighting. LTC Dillard, his voice quivering and his Adam's apple visibly vibrating in Burrow's face was saying, "George? George? The economics of war, George. The economics of war. You're trading an aircraft for 25 bodies, George. We can't afford that, George." I don't remember the end of that the conversation. Even I, a young wobbly-one knew you didn't want to be within range of an ass chewing between a colonel and major.

I will say that I remember that after the battle of Hue ended. I received a mission to carry a squad of Blues down to the edge of the Citadel where we erected a sign with a big CAV patch saying "You are entering the Ancient City of Hue Compliments of the 7th US Cavalry—Garry Owen." I thought it ironic that we, the Ninth Cavalry, were the ones to erect the sign. Why didn't they just do it themselves?

The time was approaching for me to go home, and I was becoming a real cynic. When Pratt and Mc Anally left, it meant that Larry and I were next among the pilots to DEROS. When you first came into the unit you got to know all of the guys who had been there before you. Then you remembered some of the guys who came immediately after you. But then, after you begin to lose guys, you stop really knowing the guys who came in later. Maybe this was a way to protect or insulate you from the eventuality that they might be next to die. In any case, towards the last few months I really don't remember many of the new guys.

Biggest army gun I ever saw Larry was out on a recon in the mountains to the west of Camp Evens. I was in the operations tent like I always was when Larry was out in the AO. All of a sudden I hear Larry's voice jump about twelve octaves, and hear in the background the sound of his observer's M60 working out. Larry reports that he had caught a squad of bad guys along a trail and had killed them. But also that one of them looked Chinese. There had be some intelligence reports that the NVA were being augmented by Chinese and Russian advisors. I was sent out with a squad of Blues to pick up the body, and search for intelligence.

Enroute I was briefed by the gun pilot on station. There was only one place in the entire area where a Huey could set down. Located just a short distance downhill from where Larry had killed the guys. I arrived in the area and told myself to remember to thank Larry for killing these guys in such a f*cking beautiful place. The landing area was surrounded by high ground. This was just a soup bowl of an area with triple canopy trees and jungle all around. Towards the bottom of this deep soup bowl was a little break in the trees. It was just the size of a Huey. One Huey was all that could fit. It reminded me of the hole left behind when the ARA bird went in at An Khe and Dave got Medevaced home. There was nothing that I liked about this LZ.

I came over the top and shot an approach over it. The hairs on my neck were standing straight up. I had come this far, and lived through all of this, and got so close to going home and then now, the bastards were going to get me here. Where nobody else can get in to help! Man I was pissed. But what the hell, "Live in fame, die in flame," the old cavalry aviator's oath!

I hovered down the hole. Larry was circling over the area covering me. That's comforting at least, I told myself, Larry will get the bastard who gets me. I set the Huey down and the Blues hustled up a trail to my right. I looked forward and there was a well-used trail that was wide enough for a tank to roll through. I could have dropped a load in my pants when I saw it. I could "see" it clearly in my mind, a couple of tanks rolling up the trail and topping the crest right in front of me.

I told Dale my crewchief to get ready because we may have to un-ass this thing quickly. He said that he already had a couple hundred rounds draped over his arm and had the M60 loose from the bungee cord. I knew I didn't have to tell Dale, he was ready for anything. I double checked my holster, and told myself to remember to take my M-16 with me this time. All of a sudden there was rifle firing and an explosion from a hand grenade. You could feel the concussion. I yelled to Larry over the radio, "What the f*ck is happening?" I could see at the same time a couple of Blues just beyond sight at the head of the trail backing up, moving about and firing. We were in the middle of a firefight and I knew, I knew a group of NVA reinforcements were about to come up that trail in front of us.

Larry said over the radio that one of the bad guys wasn't "completely dead" and threw a hand grenade at the Blues. I don't know where the grenade actually went or where it exploded. The Blues responded immediately with automatic firing and then things went quiet. I was still watching that trail to the front waiting for the tanks to roll up.

Shortly after, the Blues reported that the dink did look different, and that they had recovered a large caliber weapon. A couple of the Blues carried back a big long gun and put it in the back of the aircraft. I looked back at the gun as they put it in the aircraft on the right side, but I couldn't identify it.

Saber 6 was on station by now asking me what kind of a weapon I had. As best I remember, I reported: "Six, this is Three-Seven. I don't know 6, but it's the biggest f*cking army gun I ever saw." He laughed, Larry repeated the report and laughed, and that's the way the ops log read when we got back. And that was the truth; that was the biggest damn army gun I ever did see.

They carried the body of the Chinese looking dink back, put him on board and we came out of there. I was never so happy to leave a LZ, and get the hell out of an area. Some other authors have described the activity differently in their books, saying the grenade bounced through my aircraft. I won't argue with their recollections, I don't remember a lot of detail stuff. I know there was grenade thrown at us and it exploded close to us. I don't know if it came through the compartment or not. I do know the grenade was close.

When we got back to Evans, we laid the guy out alongside the aircraft. Folks from squadron and, I think, the G2 (intelligence) shop came by and looked at him and inspected the documents he had on him. They decided that he was not Chinese. He was a just a big North Vietnamese. They also identified the gun. Man that thing was big. It had to have been five feet long.

When the crowd left, we delivered some mail to Charlie.

Tempo Change The pace of the unit began to change. I don't really know why or what caused it. I don't know if the weather, the terrain, the enemy situation, or the politics of the operation was the cause. All I know is that the Blues weren't going in as often as we were accustomed. There weren't as many village sweeps or going in on ground recons based on intelligence reports. I have heard many years later that a few of the times we sent the Blues in was just to keep their edges sharpened, and not because of some report. Most of our work was directed towards securing downed aircraft and crews.

Of course another reason for the tempo change could be that we were undergoing aircraft transition and bringing in both the new gunship, the AH-1 Cobra, and scout, the OH6 Cayuse. These were to replace respectively the tried and true Huey UH1Bs and Cs, Iroquois, and the OH-13, Sioux.

Or it could have been, just personal overload and fatigue. At this point I was getting short, so I guess the newness was over and things just dragged on.

Or maybe a combination of all of the individual issues made this period a really bad and slow time for me. I was beginning to become apprehensive as well. I began to think for the first time that I may make it home after all. The thought seemed foreign to me. And I was scared to think about it, because I was afraid that by thinking of going home I might jinx myself and take a round the next minute. I had all the trappings of a short timer. I had my short timers calendar which was a checkered and numbered drawing of a red carpet leading to a big ass plane. Each checkered block contained a number from 99 to 0, and represented the number of days you had left before you got on the big ass bird and flew to the land of the big PX. I had my FIGMO (*F**ck-it *I Got My O*rders) sign up as soon as I got my assignment instructions telling me I was to go Fort Wolters Texas as a flight instructor. I had sent home copies of the humorous letter announcing to everyone to everyone that I was coming home and get ready. I had all those things, but I didn't feel comfortable, or confident that I was really going to make it.

Home was a scary, abstract place for me. Yeah I have been actively planning the wedding with Snooks. Actually she was doing the planning and I was doing the dreaming. But I hadn't thought it really through with all of the things that needed to happen. I mean, I didn't own a car! I never have owned a car, nor has my mother. How the hell can I do this, get married, and move to Fort Wolters all in a few short weeks out of Vietnam? Was I really going to get married in just a few more checkered squares on the calendar? Is Snooks really there for me?

Home. After almost 9 or 10 months in Vietnam and B Troop, could I really be going home? If I do go home, what about all the guys in the Troop I am leaving behind? Could my leaving jeopardize or jinx them? Home? Home was an incredibly hard and scary concept to comprehend; so I think I just put it out of my mind, and had another ambient beer from the case under my bunk.

Night Medevac A few nights after picking up the biggest Army gun I had ever seen, Nubs Hirning our Blue Platoon leader came into the tent and said that there was a ground unit who had wounded that needed to be evacuated or they would die. He said the weather was too bad for Medevac to launch. And the highway, as we all knew, was not secure at night. He asked if anyone would volunteer to give it a try. The weather had been shitty all day, and got worse as the night came in. The ceiling was really low. I asked Mike Covey if he wanted to try it. "Why not?" he said and grabbed his stuff. As we left the tent and hit the dark foggy air, I knew this was going to the start of a very long and a very hairy night. At the operations tent Larry came to me and insisted that he go with me instead of Mike. His rationale was, we lasted this long together, and they can't get both of us at the same time, much less in the same aircraft. Mike was okay with Larry taking his place, and he returned to the lift tent. He didn't seem too disappointed at not going.

We took off with a gun ship in formation but had to come back immediately. We ran right into the soup as soon as we picked up. We went back to the operations tent and tried to figure out what to do next. We determined that if they could fire artillery flares along the highway, all the way to the unit and back, we could maybe see the highway, and fly slowly right over the highway to get there. Larry knew the area well enough to lead us from the highway to the unit's locations. Sounds real stupid today; didn't sound much smarter then either. But following the flares was the only answer we had at the time.

They fired the artillery flares to light up the road, and we slowly flew down the highway low level. I don't remember all the particulars of the flight. I know we were on the artillery's frequency and talking right to the guys who were directing the fire. Sometimes the flare would burn out and it would get black—really black. I mean you couldn't see anything. We would slow the Huey and almost pull it to a hover expecting to run into something any second or come falling out of the sky because of vertigo. We also had a couple of duds that didn't illuminate at all and it got really dark. The cockpit was tense all the way. We didn't really have much going for us except for the artillery lighting the way with flares. We were of necessity flying slow and higher than we normally would to avoid any antennas or wires, but not high enough to make it hard for Charlie to hit us. We were lit up to ensure the gun bird didn't run into us. If the bad guys wanted us and we were out there, we were theirs.

It seemed like forever but we made it to the unit. On final they popped a flare and blinded me as I came to a hover in the LZ. I made a go around. I remember flying low level over a rice paddy field, as the gun made a run. I don't know if he landed and picked up the wounded, or I went back in and picked them up (I think so, but I don't remember.) I don't recall all of the stuff on the way back. I know we had the flares again; and the return was a slow flight hover back to base. I think we got them to the Medevac pad and took a truck back to the troop. I do know two B troop aircraft accepted a challenge one night in Vietnam. And with the help of Squadron headquarters and a US Artillery unit some US soldiers lived to see the next morning. And Larry and I were two of the pilots that made it happen.

About seven years ago now, I ran into the operations officer who was working at squadron that night and coordinated the operation. Doug Wood had been in B Troop but then was transferred to Squadron. He said that he had written and published the story in the VFW magazine about that flight from his point of view. He said in his article that in order to fire that much illumination he had to request permission to dig into the Division's reserve of illumination. He went on to say that when we touched down at Evans that there was only one round of illumination left in the division reserve at that artillery base. They had committed the division's reserve of illumination on this mission. And we used almost every round of it. This says a lot about the 1st Cavalry Division's commitment to each of its cavalrymen from the Division to grunt.

When we got back the Ol'man sent us to supply to pick up a case a beer a piece and to sleep in the next day. I don't know what happened after that. Things returned to normal after Tet. Jack Craft was getting ready to become an aircraft commander himself. I guess I knew how Jim Pratt felt when the came for me to take my own aircraft. I did as Jim did before. I let Jack make most of the decisions and I left most of the work to Jack to make sure he was comfortable. I backed him up as necessary, but flying was becoming his show. Jack was a good pilot and great guy. I respect him immensely.

Top came to me a few days later and said that the ol'man said to send me on R&R. I told Top I had already gone on R&R and besides the only place I'll go to is Sydney. (I knew this was an impossible mission. Sydney was the best place for R&R and those slots were always taken first. And Sydney was a seven-day R&R

whereas the others were only five days. There was no way he could get me to Australia.) Top came to me the next day and told me to pack up I needed to be in An Khe the following week. I was to fly to Da Nang and take an Air Force hop to An Khe. I couldn't believe it. I was going home. Not right now I knew, but after R&R. I didn't have time to think about it. When I got back from Australia I would have less than a ten days to go before I would rotate to the States. And with that little time I wouldn't be allowed back in the field.

I packed my stuff, said bye to the guys and jumped in a Huey. I flew myself into Da Nang. Nobody was going to screw this flight up. The crew consisted of Jack Craft, Dale and me in Baby Snooks II on my flight to Da Nang. I flew myself, to be sure. On arrival, we quickly said our goodbyes quickly on the ramp and I went into the passenger terminal. I don't really remember the flight down to An Khe. I remember being back in Sydney. I had taken my first R&R to Sydney in October or November. I was on the third plane load of GIs to go there on R&R since World War II. Sydney was a great R&R, and I really needed it back then.

The second trip was nice, but not as nice as the first. I guess, too many things were happening all at once. I was getting anxious about leaving Vietnam. Perhaps I had adapted too well to being in combat. Was I really going to make it through the year and come home alive? That was hard to believe. And what about the wedding? I hadn't really been able to think it though seriously for a long time. I mean I wanted to get married to Snooks. Nothing had happened to change my mind, but a lot had happened to me that I wasn't sure of much anything. I think I experienced more fear, anxiety and uncertainty over going home then I had on the way over.

In retrospect though, the R&R did get me out of the hot seat. We had just begun to work to the west of Camp Evans and in the A Shau Valley. Things were heating up pretty badly. When I returned from R&R and arrived back in An Khe I got word that

Fred Mc Murray, one of our scout pilots had been shot down in the valley and was missing. They got his observer out but couldn't find Fred. The area was so hot and the time was so late in the day, they didn't insert the Blues to search for Fred. (It hurts to writes that, even after so many years.) The next day, when the Blues got in there they found Fred's chest protector propped up against his helmet, like we always did when we got out of the aircraft, thus they surmised he survived the crash in pretty good shape. They also found one boot mark in the dirt heading towards a stream. They think he was captured and carried off by the NVA. On my second tour I flew with Fred's brother-in-law. Fred was a good man and a great guy.

A lot of stuff had happened between R&Rs and I became focused on the possibility of being able to come home. I felt good to be in Sydney. And it was good seeing some of the folks I had met on the first visit and seeing the sights again. But it didn't feel quite the same. I think I realized I had grown up! I had changed, and I was going to go home soon.

Chapter Fourteen

We gotta get out of this place—if it's the last thing we ever do. . . .

I got back from Australia and tried to catch up on what the troop was up to. I wanted to go back to Evans and see the guys one last time, but was told no! Until about two months earlier it would have been okay, but Bobby Zahn and Mac screwed that up. Seems they got a ride headed up to Evans a couple of days before they were to leave. As they were riding along in the back of this Huey-fat, dumb and happy—the aircraft was taken under intense ground fire that killed one of the pilots immediately and severely wounded the other pilot. Bobby and Mac were just riding along in the back and totally unarmed. Mac immediately reached around the dead pilot and gained control of the aircraft. At the same time Bobby broke the safety wire on the two red handles on the back of the armor plated pilot's seat that allowed him to tilt and tip the seat backwards where he could pull the wounded pilot out of the seat. Once out the crew chief began life sustaining medical aid, as Bobby righted the seat and got in. He took control of the aircraft as Mac located the red handles on the copilot's seat and removed him. Together Bobby and Mac made a bee line for the nearest medical aid station.

When they finally got up to B Troop they had only a short time to tell us what had happened. They grabbed a ride back to

An Khe on an Air Force Caribou fixed wing tactical transport aircraft. Because of this close call the SOP was established that once you went to the rear for DEROS you are prohibited from returning to the field. So, instead of going forward to say goodbye to the guys as I wanted, I signed out of the rear detachment and went to the Division's holding detachment where soldiers completing their tour were out processed from the Division and transportation home was arranged.

The place was like old home week. Each day a couple or so classmates would check in ready to go home. Al De Mailo, Bob Edwards, Bones Bradley, Larry Brown, Wiley Hazelwood, Bruce De Laurantis, they each were warmly welcomed back to the group. Everyday was a good day. There we swapped war stories about what had happened, and toasted those of our classmates who weren't as fortunate as we were.

But we had nothing to do, but wait for our final orders to go home. We would get up and have breakfast. We would go to the club as soon as it opened and drink beer. Sometimes we would go downtown to the "city" and take a steam bath and massage, or buy a souvenir. We became a pretty big crowd and a bit unruly. One night we were all throwing the bull and telling war stories about flight school and The Fish asked me if I remembered the night when we wired everyone into their rooms! Kerry Denison almost went berserk screaming, "you two did it? You sons of bitches, I swore I'd kill you." Kerry was still hot about it. He finally calmed down. But from then on whenever a new classmate would show up in the depot, Kerry would tell them who wired the doors shut. And the story telling would go on.

I don't know what we really did, or what the straw was that broke the camel's back but we were told one day on no uncertain terms by some major to go to this personnel building and out-process immediately. We went there only to be informed by this clerk that the division policy was to not out-process anyone on the last three days of the month. This being one of those days he couldn't do it. So we went back to the club.

We hadn't finished our first beer when the irate major came back screaming about us not following his orders. We told him what had happened and he became even more irate. He yelled that we should go back there and he would have them out process us. Further if anyone stood in the way of the out-processing we were to hold our ground and call him. The situation was really pretty funny. We would go to these places to out process and the clerks would tell us "no" and then we would stand there and call this guy. The clerk would get on the phone say "yesssir" a couple of times then hang up. Then he would start out-processing us. Many of the clerks asked us what we had done? We didn't know how to answer that question. We just said 'We're CAV pilots."

I guess it is safe to say that we got thrown out of An Khe. We left that afternoon for Cam Rahn Bay where we would wait to board the big ass bird and fly to the Land of the Big PX. We ended up spending the night there and getting out the next day. The Fish, Larry and me were on the same plane. As the plane lifted off a big cheer came from the passengers. As the pilot announced we were leaving the airspace of Vietnam another cheer went up. Al broke out a can of Coors he had carried over on our plane 12 months earlier. He popped it open and we each took turns drinking it. Coors doesn't taste too good unless it stays refrigerated, but this one was the exception. I conned the stewardess into letting me say over the loudspeaker "If you ain't CAV you ain't shit." And Larry did what Larry always did. Somewhere over the Pacific in the darkness of a sleeping cabin full of Vietnam veterans, Larry dropped his drawers and mooned the plane. We promised the stewardess that we wouldn't do anything else if they let us perform those small rituals. We had promised ourselves on the flight to Vietnam what we do if we made it back. And now that we had fulfilled the promise, we were satisfied enough to quietly ride out the remainder of the flight. The flight was long and numbing. Throughout it Larry would look at me and we would give each other that little smile that we had made it. Unbelievable! My mind raced from one moment and one place to another place and another time. From thinking of home and growing up and the people in my life then to the things and people in Vietnam, to the people in my future at home, to the guys and their future without me. Over and over the mind raced from topic to topic. Never an answer, just questions, and questions on questions. I was trapped on this long and tiring flight. I couldn't believe I was really enroute home. I tried to picture what home looked like. Again the mind raced and things would get blurry.

Arriving at the Seattle Tacoma airport, Fish, Larry and I raced to find an open bar so that we could have our first drink on US soil together. We found one preparing to open. We conned the guy into serving us before the appointed time so that we could have a drink before we had to split up and go our separate ways. We had our drink and our toast, hugged each other and went our separate ways.

The flights from Cam Rahn Bay to New York are mostly a big blur. I was tired and wired. On the flight from Seattle we stopped someplace enroute. On the last leg of the flight I was sitting alone by the window my mind racing again but this time the thoughts were trying to visualize arriving in New York. I didn't know what to expect. Shortly after an enroute stop in Chicago, this really pretty stewardess sat down and we chatted for some time. I enjoyed talking with her she was nice. But oh how surreal the moment. Twenty-four hours ago I was in Vietnam wondering if I am really going to live to complete the tour and now I am talking to this stew who is being so sweet and not knowing what to expect at the airport. And, was this for real? Or is this a dream?

I came off the airplane and was met by my entire family and Snooks. My nieces and nephews were there. What a great time to see them all. And they were real! And they were happy, and I was happy. Tired and wired, But happy. Not content or relaxed, but there among the faces and people I had known. It felt great to be home. I began to feel again. There was a lot to do though, I knew. I was getting married in less than three weeks and we needed to get a car, and get tuxedos, and do all sorts of things.

We went to my Mom's place where we partied all night. Being with the family again was great. They looked at me when they thought I wasn't watching and I know they had lots of questions. But they didn't ask them, and I didn't answer them. I did tell some humor, but not much. This was home and I wanted to enjoy being with them. We had a good ol'Irish party! My brother Dave fell asleep on the floor of the only bathroom in Mom's new apartment in Staten Island. When Snooks had to use the bathroom, Dave advised her to "shut your eyes and it will be all right."

The next day, Snooks and I went over to Hannah and Bill's house. Each Christmas Bill would decorate the big almost forty foot tree in there front yard with lights and ornaments. After the holidays he would take them down. This past Christmas he decided to leave them up until I came home in April. The local newspaper followed the story and had a reporter there when we showed up. He took a picture of me looking out the window at the lighted tree. Sister Edmunda Marie, my 7th grade teacher at Saint Michael's used to warn Tommy and me "Flanagan, Jennings, we'll see your names in the newspapers someday" if we didn't change our ways and be good. I thought about her when I saw my name and picture in the paper the next day. I was tempted to find out where she was and send her a copy of the paper with a note telling her that she was right again.

In the days that followed the wedding plans came together. Snooks and I would go to Staten Island where Bill and Hannah would take us for our wedding license. I would go to Dave and Noreen's house to visit for a few days and pick out a car from one of Dave's friends. Dave and Noreen had a party where I met several of their friends. One couple was into the peace movement and invited me to a rally the coming weekend. I didn't really know what was happening in the movement and told them I would if I was still in Deer Park. Luckily we got the car quickly and went home the day before the rally. Returning to Staten Island I would get with the groomsmen and get our tuxedos, etc.

Everything worked out fine. Snooks had done a great job. The wedding ceremony went off very good with Father Rod performing the ceremony. The reception went fine and everyone had fun. Snooks did a great job planning all this. Looking back on this period of time I believe I was really in a daze. There was so much to do and so many emotions. I wondered what would have happened, had those last couple flights had turned out differently. We will never know if they would have still had the party.

A week after the wedding I left New York and headed for Mineral Wells Texas. I drove our brand new, cavalry yellow, 1968 Ford Mustang convertible, with a homesick bride and a carsick dog. This was going to be a long trip. And that dog was hyper to begin with and being cooped up in the pet carrier he was really hyper. The dog, Jody, and I never really liked each other. But he was faithful and protective of Snooks.

Traveling down the interstate on the first day of our trip with the radio on and the window wide opened, a potato chip bag or something of the sort blew up from the roadway and wrapped itself around my left outside rear view mirror with a loud "WHAP!" It sounded like, and felt like, a round hitting the door of the Huey. My heart jumpstarted. My mind sped up, a gigantic shot of adrenaline shocked my system and I began to take evasive action. I was confused! Really confused as I tried to make sense of it all. I tried to figure what the hell was happening, and determine where I was? All this happened in less than couple of microseconds. Snooks jumped and yelled, and I saw on her face utter shock, surprise and maybe even fear. This too added to my bewilderment. What is she doing here when they're shooting at me? I finally realized what had happened and regained some sense about myself. I apologized to her for my reactions and said I was sorry. She said okay, but sort of looked at me funny for a while. I am not sure what was running through her mind at the time, but I feel quite sure it had something to do with questioning whether she did the right thing in marrying me.

We arrived at Fort Wolters, Texas and stayed at the local Holiday Inn in Mineral Wells. This is the motel where the preflight classes would stop by on the way home from the stagefields and ceremoniously throw each of the classmates who had soloed that day in the pool. The first few days we spent getting in processed. We got her a military ID card and showed her how to use it to get in to the PX and commissary.

One night after we had gone to bed, one of those famous Texas thunderstorms snuck over the town and positioned itself right over our room of the Holiday Inn. All I know is I heard the mortar come in disguised as the thunder, and explode right next to me. I awoke to find myself standing at the foot of the bed not knowing which way to run. I glanced up and looked into the terrified face of my wife, as she bolted straight up in the bed. I didn't know which way to run to the bunker. And I couldn't find my gun. I couldn't find my helmet. I couldn't find anything! And what the hell was she doing here? My heart was pounding; my mind was racing; and I was confused. Snooks looked at me and said "It's okay hon, it's only thunder." She was right; the noise was only thunder, and everything was all right

There were no bands or parades when we came home. One moment you are in the heat of Vietnam, the next after a very long plane ride you are back home with your family.

We met up Jim Pratt and Bobby and Bonnie Zhan just as soon as we got in to Mineral Wells. They gave us the low down on Fort Wolters from a permanent party point of view. They advised that the waiting list for on post quarters was a few months and that the quarters they had for warrant officers weren't that good. Bobbie and Bonnie had bought a mobile home and moved into a new mobile home park that promised to have all the amenities anyone would ever want, to include a pool. Snooks and I went to the mobile home dealership and selected our new home. A beautiful 2 bedroom, bath and a half, fully furnished 12 x 60 foot mobile home. We had it set up in the same park as Bobby. Pratt followed suit buying a smaller 10 x 50-foot bachelor model. He also moved into El Rancho Estates. In fact his trailer was the row behind and to the south of our trailer. Bobby was a couple of rows ahead of us. Soon after Wonder came home and bought one like Jim's. Next Jere Anderson and Rich Harris moved in a couple of rows behind us. The park almost became a B Troop compound.

Each month at Fort Wolters B Troop 1/9 CAV would have a party in one of our homes, and invite whoever just returned and reported in from the troop. The monthly parties were always good even if just to see each other and reunite. It also gave us a chance to relive and I guess to talk out some of our experiences, and to catch up on the Troop's later adventures. Many of the stories told here were first said on US soil at Fort Wolters during one of these gatherings. I think these monthly get-togethers helped us make the transition from Vietnam to the real world a little easier. The parties were mainly a guy thing as most of the guys were single. Only, Bobby Zahn, Jerry Elliot and I were married. Bobby and Bonnie were high school sweethearts. Jerry and Ingrid had been married for a while and had a son, Sean, before he came to B Troop. Jerry and Ingrid lived in a rental house in the next little town of Cool Texas. Bonnie, and Snooks who were in the center of the B Troop compound must have put up with a lot of stuff from us as we readjusted to life back in the states.

My time at Fort Wolters was good. The days were spent performing flight instructor duties, trying to teach young officers both how to fly, and how to stay alive in a hostile environment. Our flight schedule was set up for alternating weeks of mornings or afternoon periods. On the morning schedule I would leave the house about 5 AM and be home by 1130. Snooks would get up and fix me breakfast and when I left for the airfield she would start her laundry. She says that many days she waited for the sun to come up so she could hang out two loads of wash. The afternoon weeks let us sleep in late. Regardless of the flight schedule the remainder of the day was spent adjusting to married life and teaching Snooks how to drive, how to balance a checkbook, and how to cook. Many times though Snooks and I would sit out in the yard with Jody, and watch the puffy little clouds grow into towering thunderstorms in the late Texas afternoons. Life was good to us.

The rest of my life story is history. The tour as a helicopter instructor pilot at Fort Wolters. Volunteering for a second tour in Vietnam after completing fixed wing school. An assignment flying airplanes for a Radio Research Company in Vietnam. A son, James Joseph, born in March of 1970 during my second tour. Accepting a direct commission to 1st Lieutenant of Armor that same year.

Returning to the States in August of 1970 we were assigned to Fort Knox where my education as an RLO (real live officer) began, and where I commanded a basic combat training company, and later served as the Battalion Operations Officer. Then back to flying in a VIP flight detachment at Fort Knox.

During this stint with the flight detachment our daughter, Kelly Anne, was born to us in April of 1974. The Army sent me back to New York State to complete my college degree; now that I was an officer I needed an education. While attending Brockport State University I joined the Capen House Volunteer Fire Company. We met some great people there who warmly welcomed us into their circle of friends and comrades. Once again I had the privilege to serve alongside some very courageous men and their dedicated wives and families. Our whole family was sad when the time came for me to graduate and we had to leave Brockport. Following Brockport I was assigned a tour with the Army Recruiting Command in Jamestown New York that sealed my fate for retiring at twenty years. I loved the people in Jamestown and we were welcomed in to the neighborhood and the community. But at that point in time, and with the commander I had, this was the worse job I ever had. I went on an unaccompanied flying tour to Korea in 1980 and 1981 following the recruiting ordeal. Returning to Fort Knox in 1981, we bought our first house and as of this writing, our only house in 1983.

In about 1984 the Army saw fit to declare Aviation as a separate branch of the Army and adopted the insignia similar to that first worn by the army aviators during World War II.

I elected to branch transfer from Armor to Aviation. I am proud of my time as an armor officer, and as an aviation officer, but I am most proud of my Master Army Aviator wings and qualification as a 1-1 aviator. 1-1 meant that I was a dual rated master army aviator and qualified to perform instrument takeoffs in zero—zero weather. During the draw down following the Vietnam War, getting flying time was difficult and a new set of rules were established which removed or reduced many of the requirements for earning the badge. I am proud that I met all of the original qualifications for the badge of the master army aviator.

Retiring in February 1986, I re-entered the civilian world. I was very fortunate to hook up with a company which was executing what was to become the most successful Defense Advanced Research Projects Agency's (DARPA) program ever—SIMNET (Simulation Networking). This program revolutionized the way the Army could train crews and units in a realistic and tough combined arms collective training environment, while proving the technology of distributed interactive simulation. SIMNET was the closest training event to real combat a crew or unit could do, except perhaps a trip to the National Training Center at Fort Irwin, California. SIMNET was a nice transition for me as I moved from an army officer to a civilian again.

It is now 2001, and I have worked for a number of Defense Contractors in support of training and simulation. Since my "graduation" from the Army I have been around the world twice, and visited many foreign countries. It is a long way from Brooklyn—a long way from Vietnam—and, a long way from lots of other things I care not to mention. But they remain and live crystal clear in my memory. I see them when I look in the mirror each day, and feel them in my heart.

If I could, I would change some of the decisions I made in my life. But I'm not sure if that would make my life or anyone else's any better.

A number of years ago Larry Brown called me telling about some new organization that he joined. The Vietnam Helicopter Pilots Association (VHPA) was its name. They were having their annual reunion in San Francisco and Larry wanted me there. I couldn't get there in the two or three days advanced notice he had given me, even if I had wanted. But Larry persisted and I promised I would meet them the following year at the Fort Worth, Texas reunion. I went; I joined; and, I love that organization. So far Snooks and I have attended most of the reunions since then. We have met almost all of the Blue pilots there at one time or another, and many of the guns and scout pilots. A few years ago some of the Blues started coming as guests. Barry Mc Alpine, Bob Lackey, Tom Afforte, Terry Young, Billy Quinn, Baby Blue Eikenberry, and Top (Paul Tyrrell) have each come at least once to the reunion. Three years ago Earl Hobbs, my first crew chief showed up. I can't tell you how great I felt when I saw him after all of these years.

It's good seeing those folks. It is like a renewal of faith for me. I am never as relaxed as I am each July 4th when I am in the company of my brothers in the 1/9 CAV. I was born in Brooklyn, but I was raised to manhood with them in the Cavalry.

This is no shit!

Acknowledgements

I want to thank all of my comrades who have contributed to keeping the war stories alive over all of these years. I particularly like to thank those who allowed me to use their personal photos in this book. Jim Pratt, Earl Hobbs, and Loren "MAC" Mc Anally. I also thank Jim Pratt for digitizing my old 35mm slides and for his work in retrieving the Army photographs from the archives.

A small number of folks read through earlier drafts of this book and made constructive and critical suggestions. My brother Dave, sister-in-law Noreen, and my nephew Bill reviewed the first draft. Patience Mason reviewed a chapter and provided some very helpful suggestions. My comrade, neighbor and true friend Joe Batistoni saw the last draft before my final write. I thank them for their help.

I want to acknowledge the help and support of my wife through all of this. Many times while I was at the computer she was outside doing my yardwork for me.

Despite all this help I know there are errors. Any errors in the book are mine, and mine alone.

I would be remiss if I didn't acknowledge several other books written by and about the about the 1st of the 9th :

· Brennan's War by Matthew Brennan, Ó 1985 by the Presidio Press
· Headhunters, edited by Matthew Brennan, Ó 1987 by Presidio Press

- Hunter Killer Squadron, edited by Matthew Brennan, Ó 1990 by Matthew Brennan
- 9th (AIR) CAVALRY BRIGADE (PROVISIONAL) COMBAT OPERATION AFTER ACTION REPORT Ó Ltc. HILBERT CHOLE (RET) 1995
- BRAVO TROOP 1ST SQUADRON 9TH CAVALRY COMBAT OPERATIONS AFTER ACTION REPORT 1 OCT 67—31 DEC 67, by LTC (Ret) Hilbert H. Chole, Ó LTC (Ret) Hilbert H. Chole 1996

Edwards Brothers, Inc.
Thorofare, NJ USA
September 29, 2011